The Goldenseal
Book of the West Virginia
Mine Wars

Articles reprinted from GOLDENSEAL Magazine, 1977–1991
EDITED BY KEN SULLIVAN

PICTORIAL HISTORIES DISTRIBUTION
Charleston, West Virginia

Libraryof Congress Catalog Number 91-66327
ISBN 0-929521-57-9

First Printing: September 1991
Second Printing: January 1995
Third Printing: March 1998

The cover illustration by Lisa George is reprinted from the fall 1987 Goldenseal.
It is adapted from a photograph of nonunion forces at Blair Mountain.

Goldenseal is published quarterly by the State of West Virginia
through the West Virginia Division of Culture and History.

Pictorial Histories Distribution
1416 Quarrier Street
Charleston, West Virginia 25301

TABLE OF CONTENTS

Introduction

*T*he notion of a GOLDENSEAL book has been around for a long time. I inherited a good start on a book manuscript from founding editor Tom Screven back in 1979 and worked with Tom's manuscript off and on during my early years as his successor. It began to look more and more like "my" book as time passed and the pool of reprintable material built up.

Tom's original idea was to pick the best material from the first five years, as I recall. This was a natural way to approach the project, and the concept was revived briefly with each subsequent five-year anniversary. Needless to say, the task loomed bigger and bigger as each such milestone slipped past. Now, looking toward our 20th birthday in a couple of years and with nearly a thousand full-length features behind us, the job looks daunting, indeed. Practically speaking, I don't think we will ever get that "biggest hits" book published.

That's where matters stood up until last fall, when the idea congealed for a different sort of book and maybe even a series. I remember that the idea occurred to me in a conversation with Carolyn Karr of Marshall University at a conference at Jackson's Mill. Professor Karr mentioned the use of GOLDENSEAL articles in classroom teaching—something we encourage—and asked whether it would be possible to assemble collections of readings around specific subjects. I don't recall that she was interested in the Mine Wars in particular, and left the meeting with the general idea of a theme book but no particular topic in mind. That emerged later, as I looked over our collection of back issues.

It became apparent right away that we had built up substantial bodies of work around several subjects. I chose the Mine Wars over other possibilities because the story is of perennial interest to West Virginians, and also because it is strongly chronological: It has a definite beginning, middle, and end. Thus, I had not only a subject and plenty of material, but also an obvious way to organize the book.

From there it was a matter of pulling the articles, researching the blessedly few photographs we'd lost track of over the years, writing the short introductions that now accompany each article, and striking a deal with a publisher. Actually, all that turned out to be a bigger job than anticipated, but the proof that it worked is the book you hold in your hands.

That's about all there is to say about the origins of this book and the idea behind it. As to the contents, I'll only remind readers that the Mine Wars were a formative experience in West Virginia history and in the history of American labor. These episodes merit as much study and reflection as any events in our past. I believe the best way to approach them is the way GOLDENSEAL approaches every other subject, by striking close to the bone, taking our testimony from the living memory of witnesses wherever possible. Let's look at the Mine Wars through the eyes of men and women who were there, illustrating their story with the best historic photographs available.

We will approach any future GOLDENSEAL books in the same spirit, should a series follow this first one. The material is on hand, certainly, for individual books around such subjects as old-time music, tall tales, and Mountain State religion. The latter is on my mind, in particular. We've published solid articles on everything from the serpent handlers on over, so I may consider a religion book next.

In the meantime, thanks to all those who made this one possible. Thanks, first, to the writers and photographers whose work appears in these pages. The secret of GOLDENSEAL's survival is our freelancers, and you'll find some of the best of them represented here.

Thanks also to Assistant Editor Debby Jackson, who put much work into researching the details of this publication, and to Editorial Assistant Cornelia Alexander, who took the manuscript through its many variations. Thanks to Tom Screven, who brought several of these articles into print originally, and to other past GOLDENSEAL staffers who worked on the initial publication of many of the others. Thanks likewise to publisher Stan Cohen, for his work on this publication and for putting a lot of other West Virginia history into the hands of readers.

And thanks, finally and most especially, to those West Virginians who lived the Mine Wars. The struggle for a better West Virginia continues and your passionate commitment is an example to those who follow.

—Ken Sullivan
Summer 1991

Part I

The Early Years
Mother Jones Comes to the Mountain State

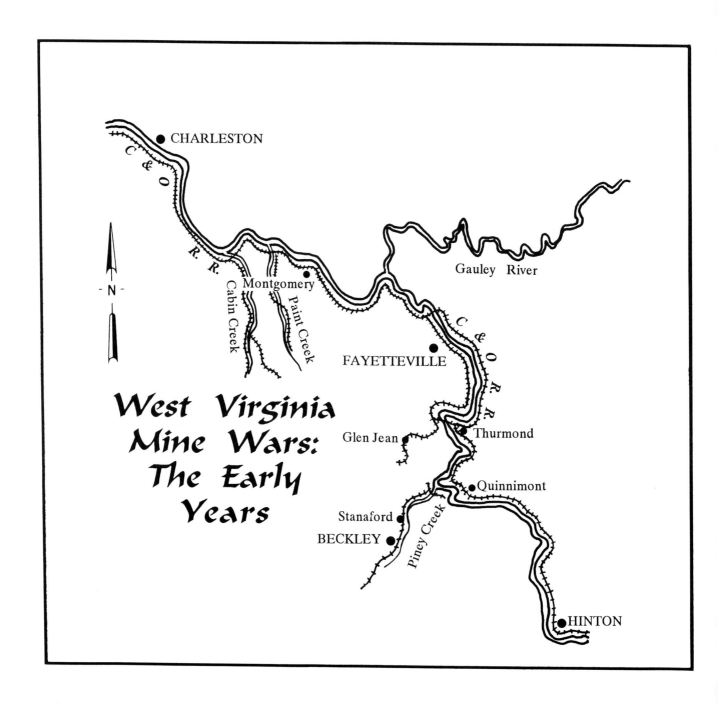

West Virginia
Mine Wars:
The Early
Years

Warm Receptions and Cordial Invitations for

Mother Jones in West Virginia

■ By Lois C. McLean

The new century brought Mary Harris "Mother" Jones to West Virginia. Known worldwide as the Miners' Angel and already the grande dame of the radical wing of the American labor movement, Mother Jones quickly became a favorite among West Virginia workers as well. She first came to the Mountain State in December 1900, and returned again and again over the course of the Mine Wars.

Although later episodes in Kanawha, Logan and Mingo counties are better known, the shooting actually began along New River in 1902. Mother Jones was in the thick of it, tramping the hills and hollows as she would on Paint and Cabin creeks in 1912 and '13 and farther south in 1919, '20 and '21.

In this article from the January–March 1978 issue, Mother Jones expert Lois McLean reviews Mother's West Virginia career from start to finish.

When Mother Jones accepted the assignment of "walking delegate" or organizer for the United Mine Workers of America in West Virginia, she knew the coal operators would not have the "Welcome" mat out for her. The pay, three dollars a day plus expenses, was no great incentive, either, for being a union organizer in the Mountain State.

In 1890 the newly organized United Mine Workers of America designated all of West Virginia as District 17 and Michael F. Moran in Wheeling was its first president. Moran frequently reported the difficulties and hazards of trying to organize the West Virginia miners but most of his union brothers in other states thought he exaggerated or got his stories from the bottle. Organizers who followed Moran, including John Mitchell, confirmed Moran's reports of operators refusing to give union representatives the time of day, of miners being fired and blacklisted for being seen at meetings or with organizers, of organizers being jumped on and beaten by "peace officers," and of the time and trouble involved in just traveling around the state.

Following the 1900 anthracite strike in which Mother Jones played a major role, John Mitchell, now president of the UMWA, announced that the union would renew its efforts to organize West Virginia. The campaign began in December 1900 and Mother Jones, along with men from Iowa, Illinois, Indiana, and Ohio, joined district president, Henry Stephenson of East Bank, in preaching the gospel of unionism. While all attempted to carry out their assignments, Mother Jones was the one hailed as "the new force" and who generated the most enthusiasm among the miners.

Mother Jones took the "walking" part of her assignment as seriously as her "delegate" duties, and the sight of the elderly white-haired woman dressed in black striding along the railroad tracks and dirt roads impressed the coal camp inhabitants as much as her words. Mother spent about a week or so that December speaking at meetings along the Kanawha River where she helped to organize new locals and reorganize old ones. She then moved into the New River field and spoke at Mount Hope, McDonald, Beury, Glen Jean, and other mining camps. She not only spoke to the miners and their families, she listened to their gripes and grievances and observed the harsh poverty of their lives and surroundings.

In January 1901 Mother Jones made her debut at the UMWA national convention in Indianapolis where she reported on the miners and conditions in West Virginia. She declared that "any man or woman who witnessed the scenes [I] saw in that state would betray God Almighty if he betrayed those people." Continuing, she stated:

> My brothers, I shall consider it an honor if, when you write my epitaph upon my tombstone, you say 'Died fighting their battles in West Virginia.' You may say what you please about the West Virginia miners being 'no good' [but] every dirty old miner out there is not a Virginian [sic]. He is very apt to be an old scab that the rest of you hounded out of your fields. I met in Virginia some of the noblest men I have met in all the country. . . . Those poor fellows realize that they have been neglected. You have not dealt fairly with them. I wish you could see how some of them live. The conditions that surround them are wretched. They have pluck-me stores

and every invention known to robbery and rascality to contend with. Why, the Czar of Russia, tyrant that he is, is a gentleman compared with some of the fellows there who oppress these people. . . . I AM GOING BACK THERE!

Mother Jones went back in May. After several speeches in the Fairmont field where she alarmed operators and politicians by urging workers to join unions, fight capitalistic combinations, and vote for government reform, she established headquarters at Montgomery in the Kanawha-New River field. Next, she took a New York City reporter, Dorothy Adams, with her on an inspection tour of the field. In her article, "Through West Virginia with Mother Jones," Miss Adams reported how the two women were met everywhere, from Quinnimont to Raymond City, by constables and squireens with injunctions forbidding Mother's meeting and speaking with the miners. She told of the ferryboat operator who refused to row them across the river because it belonged to the operator; of the miner's family that was evicted for letting the two women sleep on the floor of their company house one night; and of North Caperton, where Mother sat down on the railroad tie to wait while the constable went to Fayetteville for a copy of the law which said Mother Jones couldn't hold a meeting there. And when he didn't return, she held it anyway.

From Montgomery Mother moved to Sewell where she was joined by Illinois UMW miner, John H. Walker, who was later a president of Illinois District 12 and of the Illinois Federation of Labor. Walker often recalled incidents of their organizing on the New River. On one occasion, when they were returning from a successful secret organizing meeting in the woods, one of the men spotted a large snake on the path. Mother Jones, without losing stride, just walked past it, but the man behind her who was carrying her hat jumped so high in fright that he landed feet first on Mother's hat.

Within a year the organized and confident West Virginia miners asked for a joint conference with the operators to establish a union scale, shorter hours, and improved working conditions. The operators ignored the invitation and a strike was called June 7, 1902. Mother Jones was sent to the weak

REVISED MAP OF THE UNITED STATES

Mother Jones compared West Virginia coal operators to the Czar of Russia, and the United Mine Workers Journal *took the idea a step further.* COURTESY UMWJ

Fairmont field to work with UMW "Field Marshal" Thomas Haggerty. The operators in this field had discovered the effectiveness of court injunctions during the 1897 strike, and once again their lawyers were put to work. Injunctions were issued promptly and in less than two weeks Haggerty, his associates, and Mother Jones were arrested for violating the court orders. Accompanied by a deputy marshal, Mother Jones was taken by train from Clarksburg to Parkersburg for the hearing. When her escort tried to direct her to a hotel, she insisted she was no better than "the boys" and would go to jail. Although she shared the family quarters of the jailor and his wife for only one night, she spent part of that time writing letters to her newspaper friends. Within two weeks several papers published them with the return address, "Parkersburg, W. Va. Jail." Judge John J. Jackson refused to give a jail sentence to Mother Jones, but not to "her boys." He let her off with a lecture and a warning. Mother left his jurisdiction and the Fairmont field.

When the New River miners had answered the strike call, the operators there met and agreed to close their mines and bide their time. The next day, however, operator Justus Collins reneged, and that evening a train discharged about 40 armed Baldwin-Felts guards at Collins' operation. Their arrival angered both the strikers and opera-

tors, for Collins continued to mine and sell coal under the protection of the guards.

Following the guards, Federal Marshal Dan Cunningham and his deputies arrived, armed with guns and injunctions. By the first of August, 800 families had been evicted in the New River field. Despite pleas of sickness, death, and birth, the guards moved the miners' families from the company houses and piled their meager belongings along the railroad tracks. While their families took shelter with relatives and friends, the strikers took to the hills with their guns

A month after her trial, Mother Jones was back in the New River field and on Sunday, August 24 she was on her way to a strikers' meeting. She was met at the Thurmond railroad station by Marshal Cunningham who handed her an injunction. She looked at the paper, the Marshal, and commented, "Remember the Sabbath Day to keep it holy." Cunningham hesitated, then replied, "Six days shalt thou work and the seventh rest." Mother stuffed the paper in her black bag and continued on her way to Gatewood where an orderly crowd listened to her speech. A. D. Lavinder, a Gatewood resident, recalled that an earlier meeting in the area had not been as orderly. That one broke up when someone opened fire on the audience listening to Mother Jones. Lavinder carried Mother Jones piggyback

Coal operator Justus Collins brought the infamous Baldwin-Felts agents to town in the 1902 strike. This rifleman posed by the Collins Colliery store in Glen Jean. PHOTO BY WILLIAM TREVEY, COURTESY GEORGE BRAGG

across the creek and out of bullet range. For the small man with his sturdy burden, it was a staggering experience. Later when the two met again, they both laughed at the memory of their hasty retreat and the picture they made.

The New River strike, however, was no laughing matter. The arrogant and brutal tactics of the armed guards in carrying out evictions, as well as arresting and beating alleged trespassers and injunction violators, finally brought retaliation by the strikers. Snipers fired on guards at Caperton, Rand and Rush Run, and on August 27 a pitched battle at Red Ash between snipers and evicting guards started in the morning and continued until nightfall. Representatives of the coal companies and the C&O Railroad along with Fayette County Sheriff Daniels went to Charleston to ask Governor A. B. White for troops to put down the riot. Although he insisted that the members of

the National Guard were not strikebreakers, two days after their arrival the troops were assisting in the evictions.

By the first of October, the strike was over in the Fairmont, Norfolk and Western, and most of the Kanawha fields, but the New River men voted to continue the struggle. Mother Jones left the area to speak and raise funds for the strikers and their families. She returned to Montgomery the first of December. Editors and operators had credited Mother with the troubles in the New River field. Whether they planned her warm reception is not known, but the UMW *Journal* reported that Mother Jones, "the friend of the miners," narrowly escaped with her life from a burning hotel room in Montgomery early Tuesday morning, December 2, 1902. Her room was full of smoke when she was awakened. The fire, of incendiary origin, had started in an adjoining room which had not been occupied

for three days. This was the third fire within a few weeks at the hotel and it was suspected that Mother Jones' stopping there was the reason.

The climax of the strike occurred in Raleigh County near the county seat of Beckley. On February 21 Marshal Cunningham attempted to serve injunctions on a group of strikers who had marched from Quinnimont in Fayette County to Atkinsville (now East Beckley). Prevented from doing his duty by armed men in the crowd, Cunningham declared their action a federal offense and a riot. He returned to Beckley and asked Raleigh County's Sheriff Cook for a posse; then he went to Charleston for more deputies. The strikers meanwhile began returning to their New River home bases. A group of them spent Tuesday night with friends at Stanaford City, an unincorporated village atop a hill over the Piney Creek Gorge, midway between Beckley and

Mother Jones stirred workers throughout West Virginia. This photo shows her at Star City in June 1918. Photographer unknown. COURTESY WEST VIRGINIA COLLECTION, WVU

the point where Piney Creek empties into the New River. Before dawn on Wednesday, February 25, Cunningham, assisted by Sheriff Cook and Howard Smith, a Baldwin-Felts detective assigned to the C&O Railroad, led their posse up the mountain to Stanaford City. Strikers and residents were awakened by the invasion. In the gun battle that followed, four miners were killed, three died later, and at least 16 others were wounded. One miner, W. A. Billups, lost a leg below the knee as a result of his wound. No one in the posse was hurt.

Following the attack, all males in the area, including a 12-year-old boy, were arrested and taken to Beckley. Although participants on both sides were indicted in Beckley, the federal judge, Kellar, in Charleston claimed jurisdiction, and the prisoners were taken to Charleston. The injunction servers were exonerated, but over 200 alleged injunction violators were indicted.

Defeated by injunctions and beaten by the "Baldwin thugs," the union men retreated from the New River field. To discourage their return, the operators hired more guards, erected iron gates with floodlights, and mounted Gatling guns on their property. Many of the blacklisted and evicted miners moved into the Paint and Cabin Creek areas that were being developed and to the Kanawha field where operators signed union contracts. After doing all she could to relieve the victims of the strike and the Stanaford tragedy, Mother Jones left West Virginia. Before departing, she made a final appeal to the reorganized West Virginia Federation of Labor at their convention in Huntington to quit criticizing each other and unite.

Mother Jones traveled far and wide after she left the Mountain State, and the memories of West Virginia, Stanaford City, and "the damned Baldwin-Felts thugs" traveled

with her. Her fame as a strike leader and labor agitator made her a popular speaker with union leaders, organizers, and working-class socialists. In her speeches she often cited her experiences in West Virginia as examples of the terrible conditions that exist where labor is weak and unorganized. She urged her listeners to unite to improve their economic condition and to vote for those who would protect their political and human rights.

Mother Jones was in Montana in April 1912 when she heard about the Paint Creek strike and the Baldwin-Felts guards arriving there. Cancelling her speaking engagements, she tied all her possessions up in a black shawl—"for I like traveling light"—and headed for West Virginia. She arrived in Charleston June 9 and that afternoon spoke at a miners' rally in Holly Grove. Later there were meetings, rallies, and reunions with her old labor friends and socialist allies who welcomed her back and brought her up to date. Her friend, A. D. Lavinder, reported he wouldn't be able to carry her across creeks anymore; he had been caught by the Felts brothers, Lee and Albert, on a train "without his laundry" and their beating and throwing him off the train had permanently damaged his spine. The mine guard system they had fought on the New River had spread throughout the coalfields like a cancer eating at their organization. There were still some union men, but even the promising organization she had left on the Kanawha was affected. The depression, wage reductions, and former union leaders going over to the operators were also factors.

Their contract had expired on March 31, but they continued to work while their new officers, led by President Tom Cairns, met with operators. The union had pared its original 13 demands to two, a 5.26% increase which amounted to 2 cents a ton and union recognition with the checkoff. The operators said no deal, the miners replied no work, and the strike began at noon on April 20. The Kanawha operators reconsidered and began signing. The Paint Creek operators refused to deal with the union or grant the raise, while men who didn't return to work were fired and given notice to vacate company houses in five days and get off company property. The owners contracted with the Baldwin-Felts Agency for guards who could be legally deputized to supervise the process. With the guards' arrival, Paint Creek became a replay of the New River strike with some of the same guards evicting the same families. By May 11 "the guards were as thick as bees" on the creek and their hive was located at Mucklow, just above Holly Grove. Anyone going up or down the creek had to run the gauntlet of guards patrolling the trains, stations, roads, and coal camps.

Over the ridge, west of Paint Creek, lay Cabin Creek where the union had been driven out in 1904 and replaced with guards. The Paint Creek and Kanawha men had no intention of becoming company slaves like them. They had tolerated, for the sake of a job, company control of their hours, wages, and work places; their teachers, preachers, and doctors; their house rent, space, and location; company store prices for their work supplies, food, and clothing; and, indirectly, what they ate,

drank, and wore—even the color and material of their wives' dresses. But they would not be bossed and pushed around by armed company guards and their every move reported. The American Revolution had been for independence, the Civil War against slavery and for preservation of the Union, and their 2 cent strike became a war against the mine guards for the same reasons. On June 3 they warned the guards that the war was on by shooting up their camp at Mucklow. There were no casualties. The next day, the guards shot up the hillsides. One resident of nearby 'Taly Town was killed and one Negro looking for a lost cow was wounded; both were unarmed.

Mother Jones was glad to hear "her boys" were ready to fight for their rights; the "Angel of the Miners" would do all she could to help them. An imaginative reporter had described Mother Jones as "the Angel" during the earlier strike, but the West Virginia operators, guards, and certain prominent citizens never regarded her as such a celestial being. They didn't even consider her "a Lady," nor did they treat her like one. Mother's concern was for the miners, not the operators, whose opinion of her didn't matter. She was a woman and, in her opinion, "God made the women and the capitalists (later she substituted "the Rockefellers") made the ladies." She also believed "ladies were parlor parasites." To describe capitalists, operators, and guards Mother drew from her rich vocabulary said to have been the envy of sailors, sergeants, and mule skinners. One listener reported "she could cuss the chickens off the roost" and another ". . . a man's hat off his head." Some laughed, some winced, but all listened, for Mother Jones was a forceful speaker with a compelling message. She spoke for the miners as well as to them. As Daniel O'Connell, another "master agitator" from Ireland, once said, "How foolishly mistaken the men are who imagine that the agitators and leaders guide and direct the popular sentiment. They may echo that sentiment or give it voice but it pre-exists and operates only the stronger during its periods of silence."

The silence did not last long on Paint Creek, but the silence on Cabin Creek had been a long, almost dead one for eight years. The killing of the hated guard, Stringer, and the assault on miners led by another guard, Gaujot, on Paint Creek broke the silence

there. Mother Jones upset Cabin Creek's serenity on August 6 when she spoke to a group of miners at Eskdale. She told them it was time to throw off the chains, but first they must organize and then strike. With her help, it only took five days to do both. Next, Mother led a large miners' delegation to Charleston to request Governor W. Glasscock's help in abolishing the mine guard system and restoring citizenship to the people on Paint and Cabin creeks. The governor refused Mother's invitation to meet with her group. He did meet with a Citizens Committee who wanted him to get rid of Mother Jones and keep the guards.

Mother and the miners marched many times and many miles to bring out those miners still working on Cabin Creek. On one such occasion, they rounded a curve in the road and came face to face with a machine gun manned by Lee Felts. The group, led by Mother Jones, stopped when they saw the blockade. In his account to Major W. P. Tams, Jr., Felts told Mother Jones that he knew she wouldn't want any of her boys to get hurt, but if they came a step closer, he would open fire and Mother would be his first target. Mother Jones paused, looked at Felts, gave a laugh, and said, "Come on, boys, let's go back. That son of a bitch would do it."

That "big elephant Dan Cunningham," as Mother Jones called him, was a federal marshal and one of many lawmen to try to manage her. All failed.
COURTESY WEST VIRGINIA STATE ARCHIVES

The strike and shooting continued. The governor appointed a Strike Investigation Committee, while Mother Jones went to Washington to push for a congressional investigation. Martial law was proclaimed twice, with time out for an election. The West Virginia legislators then spent six weeks fighting over who would be their spokesman, and the operators still refused to call off the guards or meet with the union.

On Thursday night, February 7, 1913, guards aboard an armored train, the "Bull Moose Special," fired into the strikers' colony at Holly Grove. Cesco Estep, a striker, was killed as he tried to get his son and pregnant wife to shelter under the house. Guns blazed from the train, hillsides, and camp. Two days later the strikers attempted to wipe out the guards' camp at Mucklow. Mother Jones arrived from Washington on Sunday, and the next day the governor again proclaimed martial law. On Thursday Mother Jones spoke at a rally at Smithers and on her return to Charleston was arrested by "that big elephant Dan Cunningham" and Howard Smith, two leaders of the attack on Stanaford City. They took her to the military headquarters at Pratt. Mother wrote she was charged with "stealing a cannon from the military, inciting to riot, putting dinnimite [sic] under track to blow up a C-O road." Protesting that she and her friends were not there at all, Mother refused to enter a plea at her court-martial on March 8. She was a civilian and the military court had no jurisdiction. Dr. H. Hatfield, Governor as of March 4, visited Mother Jones at Pratt. She was running a high fever and the doctor prescribed a change of quarters. On May 7 she was released and went directly to Washington where she testified about conditions in West Virginia. A senate committee was appointed, despite the protests of the West Virginia senators, to investigate the charges of federal violations on Paint and Cabin creeks.

The unruly mountaineer miners finally received a hearing. Union recognition was conceded, even to the New River men, and they formed District 29. The mine guard system was not outlawed, and when another election came around in 1916 Mother Jones was back fighting. This time a truce was declared in the Fairmont field, where the Senate aspirant, Clarence Watson, agreed to eliminate the guards and deal with the union. Mr. Watson's change of heart was due to a change in the law which decreed Senators be elected by popular vote instead of legislative selection. No mean politician herself, Mother Jones agreed to speak from the same platform with Mr. Watson in acknowledgment of his generous gesture.

In Raleigh County's Winding Gulf field where new mines began opening in 1907-8, Justus Collins, formerly of the New River field, still preferred to deal only with the Baldwin-Felts Detective Agency instead of the UMWA. In 1917 Mother Jones was in Raleigh County to change Mr. Collins' mind and others'. Collins' superintendent, George Wolfe, indicated his pleasure in Mother's presence by writing his boss, "The Old Hag has announced that she will invade the sacred precincts of Winding Gulf on the 5th of May." The miners' children were excited and curious about this legendary woman and, in spite of both company and parents' orders, sneaked off and hid on the hillsides to hear her speak and to pick up a few new words.

Although seen on horseback carrying a high-powered rifle, Mother Jones' strength at this time was in Washington. Her friends and allies were working for the government and held wartime authority to influence coal production, prices, and operations which made the operators more agreeable to union recognition. As a result, miners and guards shared space on company property, but Mother Jones and her coworker, "Peggy" Dwyer, were specifically banned by one company.

Mingo, McDowell, and Mercer counties in 1919 were the last bastions of Baldwin-Felts control. The stubborn, octogenarian "matriarch of the miners" now moved into this territory with her message of unionism. While traveling by train through the enemy's stronghold, a friendly trainman warned Mother that the guards were on the train looking for her. He offered her a hiding place in the baggage car and she quickly accepted the offer. In Logan County, where Sheriff Don Chafin had replaced Baldwin-Felts men with his own army of deputies paid by the coal companies, Mother Jones was reported to have been shipped out of this territory in a cattle car.

The end of the Baldwin-Felts rule in Mingo County came in May 1920. Miners there had accepted Mother's advice to join the union, and, united, they struck against a wage reduction. The Red Jacket Coal Company gave Baldwin-Felts the job of evicting the strikers. The experienced guards, led by Albert and Lee Felts, were in Matewan when they were confronted by the mayor and Matewan Police Chief Sid Hatfield about the legality of mounting a machine gun. Accounts vary as to the firing of the first shot, but when the shooting was over seven guards, including the Felts brothers, the mayor, and two strikers were dead. Hatfield was killed the next year on the steps of the McDowell County courthouse in Welch where the scrappy police chief had been called to face charges unrelated to the Matewan affair. Felts' influence in Mercer County continued until the death in 1937 of Tom Felts who had managed the agency.

To break Chafin's iron grip the miners who threatened an armed march on Logan in 1919 decided in 1921 to do it. Having fought to preserve democracy in Europe, many of the soldier-miners felt it was time to fight for democracy in Logan County. But the most experienced veteran among the miners in their fight for democracy, Mother Jones, objected to their plans. One of the leaders said later that old age had weakened Mother Jones' fighting spirit, while others later charged with treason had more faith in their own intelligence than Mother did. She wrote later that one leader was so dumb he probably thought "treason" was a place in West Virginia. In a final attempt to stop the march, Mother Jones tried to bluff them with a presidential telegram. Miners who had benefited and enjoyed Mother's bluffs on guards, soldiers, and others suddenly were very angry when she tried one on them. Mother Jones may not have had an actual telegram but she certainly had gotten the message that troops would be used against the miners. The march on Logan was a well-known failure. Bankrupt of leadership and funds, the West Virginia miners' union began to fail.

Mother Jones' health and legendary generosity to the mountaineer miners failed too. When asked to come back to West Virginia as a defense witness for some of the leaders of the disastrous march, she refused. She did return in 1923 to ask Governor E. Morgan to release those still-imprisoned miners who had families. Morgan agreed. He was the only West Virginia governor for whom Mother Jones had a kind word.

Just months after a nationally publicized 100th birthday celebration on May 1, 1930, "Mother" Mary Harris Jones died on November 30 at the age of 93. In her auto-biography published in 1925, Mother Jones had promised: "When I get to the other side, I am going to tell God Almighty about West Virginia." In 1932 Congress enacted the Norris-LaGuardia Act, which recognized labor's right to organize and limited the use of injunctions in labor disputes. In 1935 West Virginia, at last, outlawed the mine guard deputies. Finally, somebody listened to Mother Jones.

Militia camp scene at Paint Creek.
COURTESY RICHARD ANDRE

Mother Jones in a rare moment of rest.
Date and photographer unknown.
COURTESY WEST VIRGINIA COLLECTION, WVU

Mother Jones in Court

Act I, Scene 3, from "Brimstone and Lace"

■ BY BOB AND CAROLE DAMRON

Mother Jones's 1902 courtroom clash with Judge John J. Jackson of Parkersburg highlighted the emerging class conflict in West Virginia. Mother was proud to represent the burgeoning industrial work force, while Judge Jackson, of a settled northern West Virginia family and one of the founders of the state, stood for the established aristocracy.

Their encounter, a fleet but dramatic moment in the state's labor history, was the basis for a chapter in Jones's autobiography and the following scene from a play by Bob and Carole Damron. This article is reprinted from the October–December 1980 GOLDENSEAL.

*I*n June 1902, Mother Jones was arrested while addressing a miners' rally in Clarksburg. With five others she was taken to Parkersburg, where they were brought before the Federal Court. As on other occasions, Mother quickly took control, turning the courtroom into a podium for her own views and poking sly fun at the proceedings. But this time she found a judge she could admire—a "human judge," she called him—and left the court with an unusual respect for the administration of justice.

This excerpt from the play "Brimstone and Lace" is based on Chapter 7 of *The Autobiography of Mother Jones,* third edition, published by Charles H. Kerr Publishing Company and the Illinois Labor History Society in 1976. "Brimstone and Lace" was first published in 1976.

ACT I, SCENE 3

Prosecuting Attorney: *Your honor, officials of the court, citizens of the State of West Virginia (nods to each respectively) . . . it is my duty as an officer of these proceedings to initiate contempt charges against the co-defendants for violations of injunctions issued and served by this Federal Court. Let it be known that the defendants, self-proclaimed union agitators and non-residents of* said state, have willfully disrupted the harmonious operations of coal mining business in the Fairmont and Clarksburg districts. Let the records of these proceedings show that upon receipt of this court's orders forbidding such activities at or near the private property, the defendants flagrantly ignored the request to cease and desist and were arrested in open violation of the court's injunction. The prosecution contends that since their arrival in our state, it has been the sole purpose of the defendants to create industrial turmoil in our state by any number of subversive methods. And the prosecution intends to prove that the defendants have publicly advocated the use of violence for the purpose of work stoppage in said areas. (Crowd hub-bub) With Your Honor's permission . . .*

Judge: *Certainly, Mr. Prosecutor, proceed.*

Pros. Att: *The prosecution calls to the witness stand Mrs. Imogene Franklin. (Woman enters, appearing gaunt and self-conscious. Judge administers the oath in a monotone; the witness barely audibly says "I do.") Mrs. Franklin, I shall inform the Court that you are the wife of a coal miner and a resident of Monongah, West Virginia. Is it true that you have been present during so-called labor rallies in your community?*

Carolyn Perry as Mother Jones.
PHOTO BY TOM EVANS

Judge John J. Jackson and Mother Jones made formidable adversaries. He was one of the few high officials of whom she formed a favorable opinion. JACKSON PORTRAIT COURTESY WEST VIRGINIA INDEPENDENCE HALL; JONES COURTESY WEST VIRGINIA COLLECTION, WVU

Witness: *(Meekly) Oh, yes sir, several times, sir.*

Pros. Att: *And while in attendance did you see any of the defendants here today at any of the rallies?*

Witness: *I seen ever' one of 'em. If'n they wasn't a-yellin' from the back of a wagon, they was handin' out that hate litter-chure to ever' man, woman, and child in sight.*

Pros. Att: *Yes, I see. And Mrs. Franklin, during the course of one of these gatherings, did you ever hear any of the speakers make remarks that shocked you or made you fear for the lives of your family?*

Witness: *Oh, my, yes. At one meetin' that terrible, cursing old woman told all the strikers to take their guns and go down in the mines and shoot every miner who wouldn't quit work and join them.*

Pros. Att: *What was your reaction to this, Mrs. Franklin?*

Witness: *Well, you see I was on my way to the store when I heard the ruckus. I became very fearful 'cause my husband Jim was workin' his shift in the mine at that time. I knew Jim wouldn't quit work 'cause he's never missed a day so long as he's been workin', an' sir, he's got too many mouths to feed to join up with them roustabouts even if he'd a-had the notion.*

Pros. Att: *Thank you, Mrs. Franklin, you have been extremely helpful. You may step down. (She exits with bowed head. Crowd stirs.)*

Judge: *These are serious allegations, Mr. Prosecutor. The obvious reference to the defendant, Mrs. Mary Jones, is an extraneous issue in these present proceedings. However, the court chooses to question Mrs. Jones at this time for points of clarification. The Court calls Mrs. Mary Jones! (She struts in unaided, head held high, smiling to the audience. The oath is administered in the*

same monotone — Mother replies for all to hear "I most certainly shall.") We have heard testimony that you have advised miners to use violence to stop work in the Clarksburg coalfields. What have you to say to these accusations?

Mother Jones: *You know sir, that it would be suicidal for me to make such a statement in public. I am more careful than that. You've been on the bench 40 years, have you not, Judge?*

Judge: *Yes, I have that.*

Mother: *And in 40 years you learn to discern between a lie and the truth, Judge?*

Pros Att: *(jumping up and shaking his finger) Your Honor, here is the most dangerous woman in the country today. She called Your Honor a scab! But I will recommend mercy of the Court if she will consent to leave the state and never return.*

Mother: *I didn't come into the court askin'*

mercy, but I came here lookin' for justice. And I will not leave the state so long as there is a single little child that asks me to stay and fight his battle for bread! *(Crowd whispers audibly)*

Judge: *Let me assure you, Mrs. Jones, that this Court will never ask you to compromise your search for justice (here he scowls at the Pros. Att.). And I personally share your concern over matters of grave social importance. I am slightly interested in why you referred to me as a scab. . . . Did you actually make such a statement?*

Mother: *I certainly did, Judge.*

Judge: *(slightly taken aback) Would you care to elaborate?*

Mother: *When you had me arrested, I was only talkin' about the Constitution, speakin' to a lot of men about life and liberty; to men who have been robbed for years by their masters, and who had been made industrial slaves. I was thinkin' of the immortal Lincoln, and it occurred to me that I had read in the papers that when Lincoln made the appointment of Federal Judge to this bench he did not designate senior or junior. You and your father bore the same initials. Your father was away when the appointment came and you took the appointment. Wasn't that scabbin' on your father, Judge? (Crowd hub-bub quite loud until Judge pounds for order)*

Judge: *I figured it would be that old story. Nevertheless, the Bench is not on trial here! Please proceed, Mr. Prosecutor.*

Pros. Att: *Madam, don't say "Judge" or "Sir" to the Court. Say "Your Honor!"*

Mother: *(in pantomime distress) My goodness, who is the Court?*

Pros. Att: *Why, His Honor, on the bench!*

Mother: *You mean this old gentleman behind the justice counter? Well, I can't call him Your Honor until I know how honorable he is. You know I took an oath to tell the truth when I took the witness stand. (Pros. Att. retreats, completely flabbergasted, with crowd in uproar)*

Judge: *We'll accomplish nothing at this rate this morning . . . The Court calls for a recess until 1 p.m. If you can pull yourself together, would you kindly clear the Courtroom, Mr.*

Prosecutor? Would you remain, Mrs. Jones? I believe you owe me the time you've taken up with these theatrics. (Courtroom clears and exits. Several moments of silence as Judge and Mother remain in the same positions, not looking at each other. Judge breaks the silence). Mary Harris Jones . . . you really have quite a reputation, and I have a feeling that you have hardly stopped building it . . . You are obviously a woman of strong convictions, and even though you've totally disrupted the morning proceedings, I find myself only mildly irritated but curious about you. While rooms were reserved for you at the hotel, you insisted on accompanying your cohorts to jail. Why?*

Mother: *They were no more or less guilty than I. We deserved the same treatment. I do believe you are an honorable man, by looking at you; is it so hard to understand why I would refuse preferential treatment?*

Judge: *Perhaps I underestimated your self-sufficiency. We expected you would need more suitable accommodations. I still cannot fathom why a woman of your obvious intelligence would involve herself with the*

dangerous occupation of labor organizing. Would not your talent of persuasion be better utilized in a more womanly fashion . . . the temperance movement, for instance, or . . .*

Mother: *Judge Jackson, I am neither a torch-bearing temperance howler nor a lady of refined tastes. I have lived and worked with the exploited masses upon whose backs the industries of this country have been built. They ask only a chance to better their lives. My calling is not misguided.*

Judge: *Mother Jones, would you accompany me to my chambers? I wish to give you proof that I am not a scab, that I did not scab on my father. The reports you heard were circulated by my political enemies years ago. (Rises and reaches for Mother's hand)*

Mother: *Judge, I apologize. And I am glad to be tried by so human a judge who resents being called a scab and who would not want to be called one. I can now rest assured that you know how we working people feel about it.*

(Both exit)

Judge and Prosecuting Attorney (playwright Bob Damron) examine timid witness (playwright Carole Damron). PHOTO BY TOM EVANS

The Strike of the Coal Miners is Still On!

Help your brother to break the chains of industrial slavery!

Stay Away From West Virginia!

Present the solidarity of the working class to the machine guns and dum-dum bullets of the Coal Barons.

Men, women and children, who are fighting for human rights, need your moral and financial support!

Be not traitor to your cause!

Don't accept the job of your fellow worker, who is idle for advancing the interests of Labor!

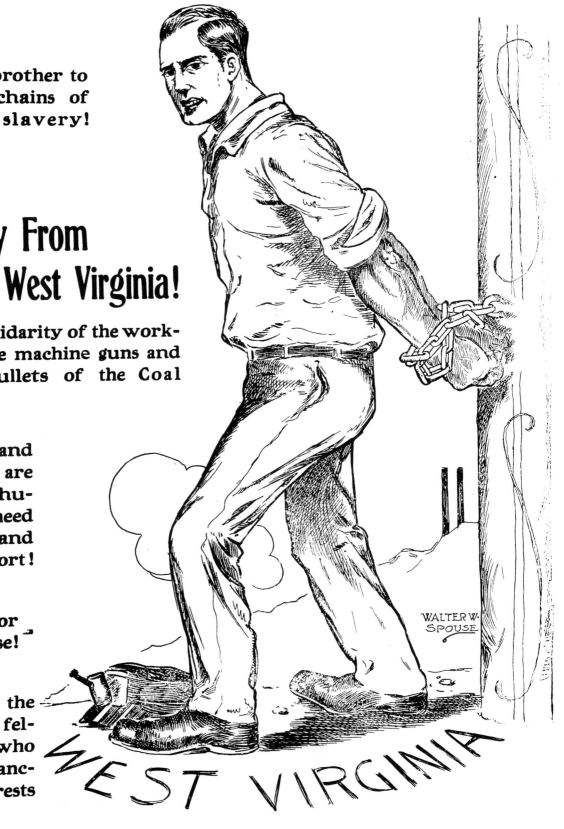

WALTER W. SPOUSE

WEST VIRGINIA

Part II

Paint Creek and Cabin Creek, 1912–13

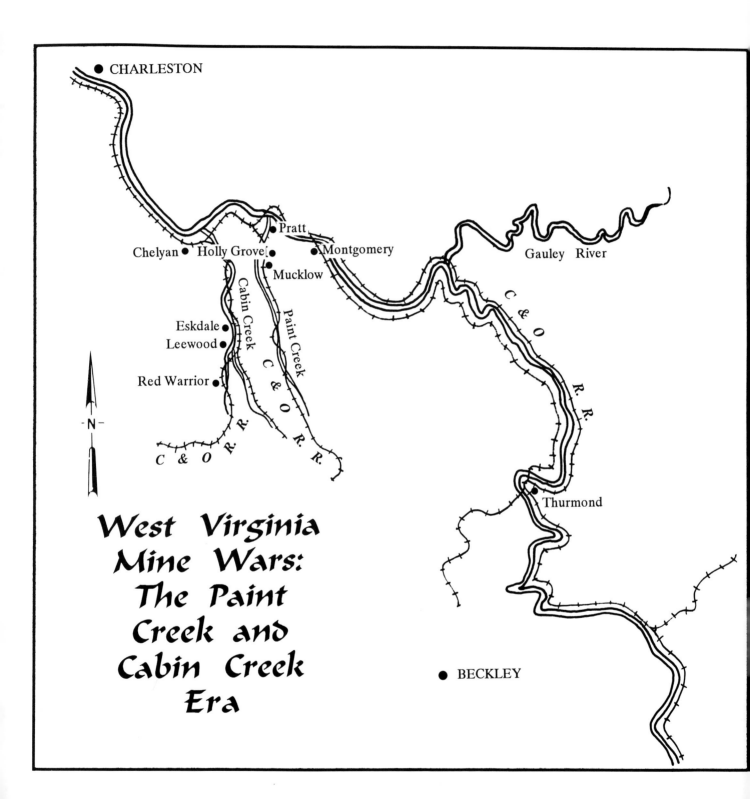

● CHARLESTON

Pratt

Chelyan ●   ● Holly Grove   ● Montgomery

Mucklow

Cabin Creek

Paint Creek

Gauley River

Eskdale ●
Leewood ●

Red Warrior ●

C & O R.R.

C & O R.R.

C & O R.R.

C & O R.R.

- N -

● Thurmond

West Virginia Mine Wars: The Paint Creek and Cabin Creek Era

● BECKLEY

Three Sides to the Story

Governor Hatfield and the Mine Wars

■ By Joseph Platania

Henry Drury Hatfield carried a famous name and a reformer's determination into office when he became governor of West Virginia in March 1913. Hatfield, nephew of Devil Anse Hatfield of Hatfield-McCoy feud fame, was the last of the Progressive Era Republicans to govern the Mountain State.

Governor Hatfield brought a full agenda for social change to the statehouse, but found himself confronted at the outset by the more pressing matter of the coal strike raging on nearby Paint and Cabin creeks. A medical doctor in private life, the new head of state promptly packed his black bag and headed for the strike zone. Having seen for himself, Hatfield proceeded to impose a contract on the warring parties. Paint Creek settled first, with Cabin Creek following later in the summer.

The Hatfield settlement represented a "third side" to the dispute, in the apt words of his daughter. It satisfied neither labor nor management but did bring an uneasy lull to the Mine Wars. Joseph Platania's article appeared in the summer 1985 GOLDENSEAL.

A blustery March wind threatened to dislodge the silk top hats of the men in the audience assembled at the old state capitol. They had gathered to hear the governor-elect, Dr. Henry D. Hatfield, deliver his inaugural address. The date was March 4, 1913, and across the nation the Progressive Era was in full swing with social and political change in the air. As a symbol of the transition, Governor Hatfield became the first West Virginia governor to ride in his inaugural parade in an automobile. But this day of orderly pomp and ceremony did not hide the fact that the state faced a grave crisis in the Kanawha Coalfield.

In the narrow, coal-rich valleys of Cabin Creek and Paint Creek, less than 20 miles from the inaugural site, martial law had been imposed for the third time by Governor Glasscock, Hatfield's predecessor. Thousands of desperate miners and their families, driven from company-owned houses, had fought mine guards in a year-long mine war. For the union miners out on strike, it had been a year of sadness, sickness, hunger, and violence.

In his speech Governor Hatfield referred to the mine war as a "flagrant contest" between labor and management. He said that a huge industrial territory was involved, and estimated that over 30,000 men were affected. Among his personal papers there is the further notation that "the year of labor trouble had cost the state over $2 million and an untold number of lives." He knew that he had inherited an open wound in this conflict.

On the day of his inaugural Hatfield expressed his desire to go into the Paint and Cabin creeks section to investigate conditions for himself. Almost a half-century later, his daughter, Hazel Hatfield Fairless, recalled the events of the time for Marshall University researcher Carolyn Karr. Mrs. Fairless recalled that her father received letters threatening his life and one threatening

Governor Henry Drury Hatfield inherited major coalfield labor troubles from his predecessor, W. E. Glasscock.
STATE ARCHIVES PHOTO

to kidnap his daughter. His military advisers also warned that his life might be in danger if he visited the strike zone. She remembered that his only reply was that "they needed a doctor." At daybreak on the day following his inauguration he made the first of several trips into the strike-torn area, carrying his medical bag and by himself.

"Right after the inauguration Father left for Cabin Creek and spent a week or 10 days up there," Mrs. Fairless recalled. "He didn't go as governor but to practice medicine. He didn't say who he was and for awhile he wasn't recognized. Everybody had pneumonia in the camps. It was a brave thing to do and created good will. He also had long conversations with Mother Jones in the camp.

"Father said that there were three sides to every story—your side, his side and somewhere in between," Mrs. Fairless concluded.

Dr. Henry Drury Hatfield, the state's 14th and, at age 37, then youngest governor, was no stranger to the coalfields and to miners. He was born on Mate Creek in what is now Mingo County, on September 15, 1875. He was the son of Elias Hatfield and a nephew of feuding Devil Anse Hatfield. Despite his family background, Henry Hatfield once told an interviewer that "all the McCoys are friendly towards me" and he had never had "so much as a fist fight with a McCoy."

Hatfield had been a doctor in the southern coalfields almost from the time he finished medical school. In his practice he had gone into shabby company houses as well as the isolated cabins of mountaineers, and often given free medical care both places. The poverty of many of his patients, among them miners who had lost their credit at the company store during hard times, made a lasting impression. Hatfield knew when he stepped off the C&O train at Cabin Creek, black bag in hand, that difficult days as a doctor and as governor lay before him.

No one had to tell the family of striking miner Cesco Estep that there was a mine war on Paint and Cabin creeks. Mr. Estep had become a casualty of that war one violent wintry night the month before the new governor arrived.

Francis Francesco Estep was a Cabin Creek miner who found six 10-hour days a week insufficient to support his family. He

also resented the oppressive mine guard system under which he worked. He decided to go with the United Mine Workers and joined the strike that broke out in April 1912. He was evicted from his company house and found shelter for himself and his family in a small frame house in Holly

Grove. In early May Cesco Estep saw his first trainload of Baldwin-Felts mine guards arrive on their way to Mucklow on Paint Creek. By summer hundreds of homeless miners were lodged in tents supplied by the union, including some living near the Estep home.

The National Guard found the adversaries in the Paint Creek-Cabin Creek war to be well armed. These are some of the confiscated guns and ammunition. STATE ARCHIVES PHOTO

The railroad permitted mine guards to outfit the train with machine guns, highpowered rifles, and ammunition. The armored train was used to transport scab workers up to Paint and Cabin creeks to work in the mines.

On the night of February 7, 1913, the "Special" had a different purpose as it carried the Kanawha County Sheriff and six deputies, plus coal operator Quinn Morton and 14 of his mine guards, into the strike zone. The sheriff had a warrant for unnamed persons, carrying the charge of "inciting a riot," to serve as legal justification for the war party.

As the darkened train moved past the tent village of Holly Grove, where armed strikers were thought to be hiding, the firing started. Sleeping families awoke to the sound of bullets ripping through their tents and houses.

The Estep home was in the line of fire. Cesco hollered to his wife, Maud, who was seven months pregnant, to get two-year-old Clifford and go to the cellar for safety. As Maud ran with the baby, Cesco was outside running toward the back. As he turned the corner, more than 100 rounds perforated the little house, with 19 bullets passing through Maud's and Clifford's clothing without leaving a scratch. Cesco was less fortunate. One bullet caught him in the face, killing him instantly in the sight of his wife.

Early the next morning Maud Estep was taken to a nearby hospital and Clifford taken in by relatives. More than 60 years later he was interviewed by Associated Press writer Strat Douthat. Clifford had come at the invitation of the West Virginia Labor History Association to attend the 1975 Labor Day picnic at Holly Grove in honor of his father.

"I was two years old at the time my father was killed," Estep recalled for the reporter. "He had stepped outside and I was in the house with my mother. She was holding me

The strike had dragged on through the summer of 1912 as strikers tried to drive the mine guards from the area. Twice martial law was declared by Governor Glasscock. On the morning of February 7, 1913, another shooting incident took place near Holly Grove. That set off rumors that the guards were going to attack the tent colony from the "Bull Moose Special" during its late run up the creek.

The "Bull Moose Special" was a steel-plated train that rolled out of the Huntington C&O shops in February 1913, consisting of a locomotive, baggage car and, day coach.

in her arms while they were shooting. She said the bullets sounded like splinters flying off the wall and there were a hundred bullet holes in the house."

"They even shot up my father's funeral a few days later," Mr. Estep reported bitterly. He enjoyed the 1975 memorial picnic and died two years later with the knowledge that his father was no longer a forgotten hero of the early struggle.

Dave Tamplin of the Fayette County town of Boomer also remembered those bloody days on the two creeks. He was interviewed in April 1973 as part of Marshall University's Oral History of Appalachia program. Mr. Tamplin had lived in Boomer since his birth in 1894 and was an independent businessman there.

"Those on Paint Creek came out on strike in 1912," he recalled. "There was a few of them that went back to work but most of them didn't. The union was strong in the Valley, but not up New River and not up the creeks. So, they were trying to organize up Paint Creek.

"No organizer for the union or any person at all, if you didn't work up the hollow, was allowed to go up through there and go on company property," Mr. Tamplin continued. "They had militia all up there. They were all practically kids around 17, 18 and 19 years old, and getting a kick out of belonging to the militia."

Tamplin remembered that a Colonel Ford was in charge of the militia. "He knew that the miners at Muckow and Mahan and those places were getting food and ammunition from somewhere else besides getting it up through Paint Creek. What was going on, the miners from Boomer and this vicinity were going up Morris Creek and over the mountains to Paint Creek and taking them ammunition and supplies.

"Nobody had any use for the militia," Mr. Tamplin said, "because they were considered mine guards in those days." He went on to compare the militia to Pennsylvania's notorious "Coal and Iron" police. "They was the ones that run the bullpen at the mouth of Paint Creek. If they caught a man attempting to go up the creek and organize, they would put him in," he added. "They had a fence around it, made of barbed wire. They'd fence him in the bullpen, kept them in there maybe for two or three weeks at a time." Tamplin credited Hatfield with recti-

fying the situation. "That was the first act that Governor Hatfield did when he came in. He sent Colonel Abe Lilly, which was our attorney general, up there to tear that bullpen down. So Abe Lilly came up to the mouth of Paint Creek and they did away with the bullpen."

John T. Walton, born in Kanawha County mining camp of Black Cat in 1904, supplies another firsthand account of the Paint Creek mine wars. Mr. Walton grew up in a series of mining camps including Mucklow, Kayford and Quarrier in the Paint-Cabin area. His father operated company stores in these coal camps. The Walton family later moved to Lewisburg and then to Huntington in 1923. He was interviewed in May and June 1976 in Huntington as part of the Oral History of Appalachia program.

"Mother Jones came into our camp on two occasions," Walton recalled. "I did see her up on the stand addressing the men one time. The other time may have been over at Smithers." Walton was aware of the revered labor leader's fiesty reputation. "They'd wrote bad things about her in the paper," he said. "Sometimes she had said these things and sometimes she hadn't."

Mr. Walton also recognized the mine guards' role in the labor war. "The Paint Creek strike had been coming up for some

time. For several months production was down in the mines and everybody was on edge and the tension was high. Finally the coal operators decided they'd bring in the Baldwin-Felts guards. Well, I think if they'd left those fellas out of there things would've been a whole lot better.

"The mine guards stayed at what we called the clubhouse at the upper end of the camp," Mr. Walton said, referring to the camp at Mucklow. "I think it must have had 14 or 16 rooms in it. It was a good-size thing and this lady ran it for a number of years. She took care of visiting officials and the guards who also ate over at the clubhouse. There were about 15 guards in all. They didn't bother anybody, of course, but some of the teenagers would hurl some very nasty remarks in their direction. The fact was, the store man was in between the company and the men all the time. You had to please the company and you had to please the people. We just kept right in the middle of the road. But the men respected my father. There was just no two ways about that."

John Walton turned in his memory to the Battle of Mucklow in the summer of 1912. "Well, about two days before the battle it seemed that everybody just evaporated from the camp," he said. "A lot of men took their families out on the train as the trains ran steadily up and down the creeks.

The troops set up their camp at the mouth of Paint Creek, near Pratt. It was here that the "tin horn" court was held. STATE ARCHIVES PHOTO

"Mr. Scott, who was in charge of the stable, took his family and went down someplace on the river to visit relatives. So Dad had to look after the mules, and on this particular day it had gotten around that there was just liable to be a mighty big battle. That morning Mother took her two kids and we crawled under the house down in next to the chimney, so that if they did shoot down that way, well, maybe we'd all be safe. Dad got up at his regular time, built a fire in the stove, and went over and fed and watered the mules. He did just ordinary things around the house and then went up to the store for awhile. In the meantime, the guards had built themselves a fortress just down the hill from the clubhouse at the foot of this little hill. They took green cross ties and stacked them so that they would have protection. They fixed it so that they had almost a 360-degree view of the camp.

"The guards had lever-action Winchesters and then they had this Gatling gun," Walton continued. "It was really a fine piece of machinery. They'd run the Gatling gun until it got hot, so hot they're afraid the bullets

would stick in it, and then they'd let it up when the other men started in with their Winchester rifles. The guards sprayed the

Hatfield in his medical corpsman uniform. He was able to use his status as a doctor to gain confidence among the miners. STATE ARCHIVES PHOTO

woods with bullets in every direction. When this Gatling gun stopped you could hear the trees splitting. They'd crack and pop like they do up north when it's cold, they say. But only one bullet landed in our yard. It was a stray."

After the strike broke out, the coal companies had protected their property with search lights and concrete forts manned by mine guards at strategic points in the narrow valleys. The operators then began to reopen their mines with scab workers lured by ads in large Eastern newspapers offering steady work at good wages. The imported workers were brought in by special trains, escorted by mine guards.

The return of Mother Jones to West Virginia was a major turning point in the conflict. She had earlier visited the state as a UMW organizer at the time of the 1902 general strike. Now the old woman was 82, and no less determined. Soon after her arrival, she rallied thousands of miners on the state capitol grounds where she denounced Governor Glasscock and inflamed her audience to arm themselves and do whatever was necessary to win their fight.

Howard Lee, West Virginia's former attorney general who is now 105 and living in Florida, reports in his book, *Bloodletting in Appalachia*, that mine guards were ambushed and killed by the strikers. Assaults, murders, sniper attacks, pitched battles and destruction of property were daily occurrences. These guerrilla activities led to the July 26, 1912, Mucklow battle that John Walton remembers so vividly. An estimated 100,000 shots were exchanged between strikers and guards. Miraculously, only 12 strikers and four guards were reported killed, although the number of dead miners may have been much higher, according to Lee.

While the Walton home at Mucklow was spared, the company store was caught in the crossfire. "They fired at the store mainly from the Gatling gun emplacement," John Walton recalled for the Marshall University interviewer. "They riddled the top of the store and later we had to put all sorts of patches on it to keep the rain out, and replace the good-size plate glasses. There wasn't a glass window or a piece of glass left. And then inside, where they hit the pine floor, one of those bullets would go down in there and there'd be a splinter stick up almost a foot above the floor.

"There were 50 to 60 shots in the store, mainly through the ceiling and roof. I think the biggest part of these fellas [the miners] were on the mountain. They had binoculars and some of them would sit there and they'd pin out a man and pretty soon they'd concentrate their fire on him. The battle lasted, I think, about two or two and a half hours. And for years after that, up on the mountain, kids would find what we called 'puddles,' or the empty shells from the bullets that the miners had used in the battle. They were quite a collector's item there for awhile."

On September 1, 1912, union miners from the north side of the Kanawha armed themselves and crossed the river to aid the strikers. Almost 6,000 men headed for the strike district. Mine guards, warned of the pending invasion, resupplied their arsenals and manned the barricades.

This was the volatile situation on the morning of September 12, 1912, when Governor Glasscock, fearing the enraged miners would wipe out the guards, declared

This front page from August 1913 deals with the different issues facing Governor Hatfield in imposing a settlement on the Paint Creek-Cabin Creek strike.

the strike zone under martial law and sent 1,200 state militia by special trains into the region. The militia seized 1,872 rifles, 556 pistols, six machine guns, 225,000 rounds of ammunition, and 480 blackjacks in the area of the fighting, according to Lee. A military court was set up and a nearby freight house was made into a jail, "the bullpen at the mouth of Paint Creek" that Dave Tamplin mentions. By the middle of October the militia was withdrawn, only to be returned a month later.

Under this second round of martial law, another military court was set up to try all offenses committed within the strike area. Miners' rights as civilian citizens were denied by a court that worked with frightening speed. Men arrested one day were tried the next, without benefit of counsel or witnesses, and sentenced to the penitentiary or to local jails the third day. As many as 30 men were tried at a time. Lengthy prison terms were handed out for misdemeanors. The judges were "laymen untrained in the law and they had little regard for the laws of the land or for the U.S. Constitution," states Lee. Mother Jones was seized by the militia during this period, for attempting to read the Declaration of Independence on Cabin Creek.

By January 10, 1913, the militia was again withdrawn and martial law lifted. In its wake, Lee comments, "the operators brought in their scab workers under military protection; mines resumed operation; and thousands of miners and their families starved."

On February 10, 1913, three days after the attack on Holly Grove by the "Bull Moose Special," Governor Glasscock issued his third and last martial law proclamation and troops were again rushed in. A new military court convened and many strikers were given jail sentences. More than 20, including Mother Jones, were handed 10- and 20-year terms in the state penitentiary.

This was the situation that W. E. Glasscock handed over to Henry Hatfield on inauguration day. The new governor was left the responsibility of reviewing the many pending convictions of the military courts. On the second day of his visit into the strike zone at a camp near the Kanawha River, Hatfield's attention was drawn to a small hut removed from the rest of the debris and the military compounds. It was here that he encountered the infamous Mother Jones and he met her as doctor as well as governor.

Researcher Karr found Hatfield's recollections of what transpired among his papers. "I noticed a soldier marching to and fro in front of the little cabin on the banks of the Kanawha River. I told the soldier who I was and inquired what responsibility he had there. He told me Mother Jones was being guarded in this little shack and when I entered I found her lying on a straw tick on the floor, carrying a temperature of 104, a very rapid respiration and a constant cough. She had pneumonia."

The new governor immediately ordered that Mother Jones be removed from the hut. "I flagged the first train and had a soldier take her to Charleston where she was placed under the care of a competent physician," he remembered.

Many years later in a Huntington newspaper interview, Governor Hatfield reflected, "When I put Mother Jones in the hospital, though, I thought surely she would die. I got some outside physicians to treat her, however, and they were successful."

Soon after his return from his mission of mercy to the strike zone, Governor Hatfield took action to bring both sides together for a settlement. He had created personal good will in the battletorn area by his visits. This was reinforced by the pardon he gave

Mother Jones was among those treated by the doctor governor. She looks peaceful enough in this photo soon after the strike, but was known as a terror of the coalfields. She poses here with friends in 1913 or 1914. WEST VIRGINIA COLLECTION, WVU

Mother Jones and all others who had been convicted by the military courts. In Hatfield's own words, "I quietly turned out of jail and the penitentiary all military prisoners who had been sentenced by my predecessor."

As expected, the operators and union leaders were unable to agree to a settlement. Hatfield himself then took over the negotiations, making his own proposal. The union remained suspicious of his contract proposals and delayed accepting them. The governor lost his patience and gave the strikers an ultimatum—"either accept it or get off the creek." He had still greater difficulty with the operators, who were openly hostile to any proposal which gave the miners the right to organize. But his demand that the strike cease within 36 hours was complied with, and both sides finally accepted the terms of the "Hatfield Contract." It was signed on May 1, 1913.

With Hatfield's help the strikers won some gains, but at a high price already paid by their own and their families' suffering. The union could now become the bargaining agent for Kanawha Coalfield miners. The terms agreed upon also included a nine-hour work day; the coal operators' agreement to the right of the miners to organize and to grant them the right to trade in independent stores; payment of wages twice a month; and roughly a two-and-a-half cent a ton increase in wages. Small boys and old men who operated the mine ventilation doors—jobs on the bottom rung of the mine system—would now receive a dollar for nine hours work.

The settlement did not bring an end to West Virginia's Mine Wars, for further blood was to be shed at Blair Mountain and other places within a few years. But the truce did bring temporary peace and a welcome respite for the troubled twin valleys of the Kanawha Coalfield. Governor Hatfield had looked at the "three sides" to the story and had found the third way right where he expected it, between the demands of the warring contenders. For his first two months in office it was a considerable accomplishment and, for the time, it was enough.

More munitions from the strike zone. Note the coal company machine guns at front and the boxes of ammunition behind.
STATE ARCHIVES PHOTO

Blood Flows on the Creeks

The Killing of Estep and Woodrum

■ By Lois C. McLean

There has never been an exact body count for the West Virginia Mine Wars, but the conflict left its dead across the southern counties. One of the best known cases is that of Francis F. "Cesco" Estep, the victim of the infamous "Bull Moose Special" raid on a tent colony set up by striking miners at Holly Grove on Paint Creek. The darkened special, an armored train built by the coal operators for the purpose of transporting scabs and mine guards, crept through Holly Grove on the night of February 7, 1913, pouring machine gun fire into the tents and houses of the community. Miraculously, Estep was the only fatality, falling dead at the feet of his pregnant wife.

Governor Hatfield's intervention soon brought a settlement on Paint Creek, but the trouble lasted longer on Cabin Creek. Cleve Woodrum died there in the union cause in July. Woodrum, a victim of infamous mine guard Don Slater, instantly joined Estep in the pantheon of mine worker martyrs. At some unknown later date the two men were also joined in another way, as recipients of matching commemorative gravestones provided by the union.

Lois McLean raised the mystery of the forgotten commemoratives in this article for the October– December 1978 GOLDENSEAL.

*I*n the hilltop cemetery overlooking Holly Grove on Paint Creek lies an unusual grave marker, a small block of hand-hewn granite with a bronze tablet mounted on its polished surface. On the tablet, in relief, is the seal of the United Mine Workers of America and these words: "Dedicated to the memory of Francis F. Estep for distinguished service and self-sacrifice in the cause of labor and advancement of the United Mine Workers of America."

An identical marker, except for the name, lies in the corner of an all but abandoned cemetery located between the railroad tracks and a burned-out stone building at Eskdale on Cabin Creek. This monument is dedicated to the memory of Cleve Woodrum.

The monuments mark the graves of two striking union miners who met identical fates. Both were shot and killed by Baldwin-Felts mine guards during the 1912–13 strike on Paint and Cabin creeks.

According to a family Bible, Francis F. Estep was born at Hudnall (Kanawha County) on October 15, 1882. The firstborn of Reuben and Liza Jane Estep's six children, he was christened Francis Francesco but early acquired the nickname "Cesco." In 1906 Cesco married Maud Gallian, born at Tuscora, Kentucky, on October 26, 1890. Their first two sons Clarence (1907) and Cebert (1909) died in infancy and were buried in the Estep family plot at the Holly Grove cemetery. A third son Clifford Allen was born on September 16, 1911.*

On March 31, 1912, contracts between miners of District 17 of the United Mine Workers of America and operators on the Kanawha River and Paint Creek expired. After two weeks of waiting for a new contract, the miners voted to go on strike at noon on April 20 if no settlement was

---

*Cesco had a son Everette by a previous marriage.

Both sides experienced tent life during the Mine Wars. This is another view of the camp of the government forces at Mucklow, 1913. COURTESY WEST VIRGINIA STATE ARCHIVES

reached. The Kanawha operators agreed to the reduced demands of their men, a 5.26% wage increase and union recognition through the checkoff system, but the Paint Creek operators refused.

Cesco Estep, digging coal at 47½¢ a long ton (2240 lbs.), ten hours a day, six days a week, could barely support his family, but even worse was working and living under the nonunion, mine guard, and spy system in effect on Cabin Creek. Cesco, who had been working at Acme on Cabin Creek, decided to go with the union and joined the strike. He had to move out of the Acme company house but, with the help of friends and relatives, he found a small frame house at the southern end of Holly Grove on the west side of Paint Creek. A swinging bridge connected the section where Cesco lived to the main settlement of Holly Grove.

On May 7, 1912, Cesco Estep saw the first contingent of Baldwin-Felts mine guards arrive on Paint Creek. The train carrying them passed his house on the way to Mucklow (now Gallagher) just above Holly Grove. By the end of the month there were over 40 guards headquartered at Mucklow and policing the Creek.

The first of June the Paint Creek

operators announced that men refusing to work on their terms would be evicted in five days and barred from company property. The guards proceeded to carry out the orders and their manners and methods did nothing to ease the tense situation. Holly Grove residents shared the strikers' anger and resentment toward the guards and offered space in their little community. Reuben and Liza Estep shared their backyard with three families living in tents provided by the UMWA, and five families pitched their tents between Cesco Estep's house and the little "dinky" road. Hundreds of others lived in tents scattered throughout the area.

The strike dragged on, and in August miners on Cabin Creek joined those on Paint Creek in a campaign to drive the mine guard system out of the creeks. Twice martial law was declared on both sides. On the morning of February 7, 1913, there was another shooting incident above Holly Grove between strikers and guards. That evening the rumor spread among the tent-dwellers that the guards were going to wipe out their colony and that the attack would come from the armored train, the "Bull Moose Special," as it made its late run up the creek.

In Cesco Estep's house at 10:30 that night, Cesco, his brother Jim, his cousin Enoch Farell, and friends Jim and Bob Fauber were talking about the rumors. Maud Estep, who was seven months pregnant and tired, decided to go to bed. Little Clifford was already asleep. As Maud Estep was untying her shoe, she heard the sound of the train and guns firing. The sounds grew louder and the men ran out the front door. Within seconds Cesco hollered at his wife to get the baby and go to the cellar. As Mrs. Estep, with Clifford, headed through the house to the back door, Cesco was outside running toward the back. Just as he turned the corner, there was a great hail of bullets from the darkened train across the creek. Over a hundred of them pierced the flimsy boards of the house, 19 of them passed through Maud and Clifford Estep's clothing without leaving a scratch, and one caught Cesco Estep in the face. He dropped dead at his wife's feet. In shock and rage, Maud Estep set her son down, grabbed her husband's gun, and emptied it at the disappearing train.

Early the next morning Maud Estep was taken to the Sheltering Arms Hospital at Hansford. Clifford was taken in by relatives

THE STRIKER'S ORPHAN CHILD

Among the many labor ballads by Walter Seacrist (see the next chapter), was one about the murder of Cesco Estep, told from the perspective of his fatherless child. The photograph shows Clifford Allan Estep, who was less than two years old when his father was killed.

My father was a striker back in nineteen and thirteen.
He was the sweetest daddy; he never treated us mean.
He worked in dark and danger, almost day and night
To earn for us a living, to bring us all up right.

We all were Oh so happy. We were so wondrous blest.
The Union issued a strike call. Dad came out with the rest
To better his condition, that he might not be a slave,
That they might have a Union, and get a living wage.

They cared no more for the miner than a cat does for
    a mouse.
They came on cold and rainy days and throwed them
    from their house.
Mothers with newborn babies, so innocent and so sweet,
Without the least protection were cast out in the street.

And as I look around me and see the same thing near,
I wonder what would happen if Daddy could be here
With some of his old buddies of nineteen and thirteen
For he could not stand to see little children treated mean.

On February the seventh, eleven o'clock at night,
The sky was clear and beautiful, the stars were shining
    bright.
The high sheriff and his gunmen up from Charleston came
And shot up our village from that fatal Bull Moose train.

My Daddy heard the shooting and rushed us from our bed
And a few moments later he was found dead.
While trying to get us to safety and find for us a place
An explosive rifle bullet had torn away his face.

Don't weep for me or Mother, although you might feel bad,
Just try to help keep alive some other boy's dad.
And when we meet in heaven, on that golden strand,
Then you can see my Daddy and clasp his blessed hand.

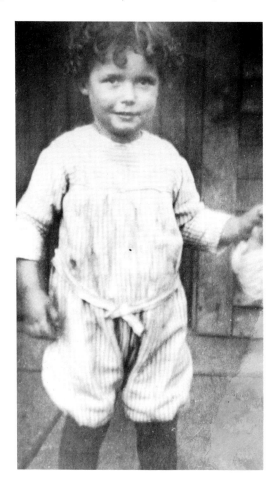

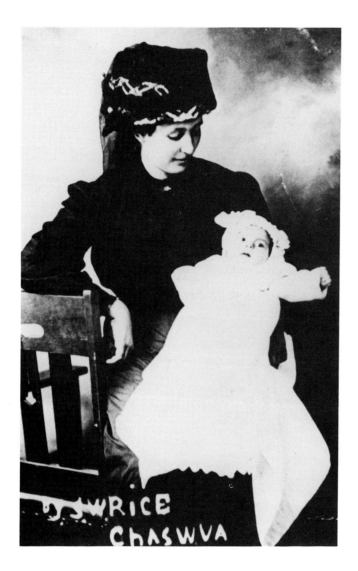

and Cesco's body was taken to the Estep family plot where it was buried beside those of his two sons. Maud Estep was unable to attend her husband's funeral but friends reported that even Cesco's funeral was marred by guards firing from the hillside into the crowd at the cemetery. These shots plus those from the train triggered the strikers' February 9 attack on Mucklow. The next day retiring Governor William E. Glasscock declared martial law for the third and last time.

On April 9, 1913, Maud Estep gave birth to a daughter whom she named Frances Francesco in memory of her husband. She never returned to the house at Holly Grove. There were no Social Security or union benefits in 1913 and Maud Estep, unable to support herself and her children, later remarried. She lived in Alloy for a number of years but after being widowed again, she moved to Greenbrier County where she died in 1955. For several reasons, Cesco Estep's children, Clifford and Frances, never saw their father's grave. After the death of their mother, both visited Holly Grove cemetery but were unable to find a marker.

Cleve Woodrum was born on October 12, 1884, in Kanawha County and was one of nine children born to Richard and Eliza Jane Brown Woodrum. In 1903(?) Cleve married Laura A. Dickens. Laura, born on Davis Creek on August 8, 1887, was a daughter of Louis and Nancy Estep

Maud Gillian Estep with her daughter, Frances Francesco Estep, in the summer of 1913. PHOTOGRAPHER UNKNOWN, COURTESY FRANCES F. ESTEP EVANS

Mine guards at Cabin Creek Junction the day before martial law was declared, September 1, 1912. COURTESY RICHARD ANDRE

The Estep family gathered for the 1975 Cesco Estep commemorative service. They include Novella Estep Green, Drema Estep, Clifford Estep—the "Orphan Child" of Walter Seacrist's song—Sadie Estep; Frances Estep Evans, and Margaret and David Steagall. Frances holds Mother Jones' purse, while David holds a picture of Jones.
COURTESY LENA ANDERSON

Dickens. When the 1912 strike started, Cleve and Laura Woodrum lived up Lamont Hollow near Eskdale with their five children, Ollie, Cleve, Jr., Ivory, Artie, and Kenneth. They were expecting their sixth child in September.

With the exception of several mines near the long hollow's mouth, Cabin Creek had been nonunion territory since 1904. To keep it that way, Cabin Creek operators hired mine guards and undercover men from the Baldwin-Felts Detective Agency at Bluefield. One of the guards, commissioned a deputy sheriff, was Don F. Slater, and had been on the job at Acme since 1904. According to Fred Mooney on page 27 of his book, *Struggle in the Coal Fields* (1967,

McClain Printing Co.), "Slater was a bruiser. He was bold, ruthless, and entertained no scruples against taking human life. He passed up no opportunity to crack the head of a striker or even a miner who dared to talk of unionism."

On August 6, 1912, Mother Jones, at the request of C. Frank Keeney, spoke at a miners' meeting in Eskdale, the oasis of independence on Cabin Creek. She urged the men to throw off the chains of slavery fettered by the mine guards. Many heeded her advice and the strike was on. As the number of strikers, guards, and guns increased or the creek, so did the attacks by both sides. On September 2, 1912, Governor W. E. Glasscock proclaimed martial law for the

Paint and Cabin Creek areas. State militia moved in, collected arms, and arrested some from both factions. Although welcomed at first, in time the "tin horn" soldiers were no better liked by the strikers than the "red neck" mine guards as they patrolled the area, enforced an 8:00 p.m. curfew, and broke up any gathering of three or more persons.

On the night of September 19 Laura Woodrum went into labor and Cleve, on horseback, went for the doctor. Stopped by a patrol and questioned, he was finally permitted to go on. It was after eight o'clock and there were lights on in the little house up Lamont Hollow as the doctor prepared to help delivery of the newest Woodrum.

Don Slater, one of the Baldwin-Felts agents on Cabin Creek, engaged in hand-to-hand combat with Cleve Woodrum. Both men died. Photographer unknown.
COURTESY WEST VIRGINIA COLLECTION, WVU

Suddenly there was a banging on the door and a voice shouted, "Turn out those lights!" Cleve and the doctor went to the door. They explained to the patrol leader that there was a birth in progress. The man insisted that they turn off the light or blind the windows; if they didn't, they would shoot the lights out. Cleve Woodrum angrily told them to go ahead and shoot but "by God, he (will) get some of them." As he slammed the door someone shot out the light. Grace Woodrum entered a semidark world that night.

After three declarations of martial law, a general election, a new governor, and two investigations, one by the State of West Virginia and the other by a U.S. Senate subcommittee, the Paint Creek operators signed

a contract with the UMWA on July 1, 1913. The strike continued on Cabin Creek.

On the evening of July 23, 1913, several men came to Cleve Woodrum's house in Lamont Hollow. Cleve said they were going "huckleberry picking," but his daughter Ivory recalled that they all seemed rather serious. Her grandparents Rich and Eliza Woodrum were there as well as Cleve's younger brother Erwin. There may have been more. The entire group gathered around Laura Woodrum's organ and while she played they sang first, "Nearer My God to Thee," then, "There's Not A Friend Like the Lowly Jesus." After a short prayer, the men began to leave. Cleve Woodrum told his daughters Ollie and Ivory to look after

the baby Gracie and asked his brother Erwin to take care of Laura.

Early the next morning there were reports of a shoot-out above Red Warrior. Several hours later Cleve Woodrum returned to the house up Lamont Hollow dead, a victim of Don Slater's gun. Following the funeral service, Cleve Woodrum's body was escorted to the small cemetery at Eskdale where it was laid to rest in free soil.

Charleston newspapers on July 24 and 25 reported the shootings as "guerrilla warfare at Wake Forest" and an "early morning riot on Cabin Creek." "Victims of striking Miners" were identified as Don Slater, Frank Ginn, and Lee Woodrum." Details were taken from Don Slater's antemortem statement given to assistant Prosecuting Attorney Frank C. Burdette. According to Slater, he and Frank Ginn, a mine watchman from Wake Forest, met Woodrum and another man on the mountain near the Wake Forest mine. All four had drawn guns. When Slater asked "the boys" what they were doing, one, identified as Lee Woodrum of Lamont Hollow, replied, "We are picking huckleberries." Hearing a gun click, Slater started for cover behind a tree. Woodrum fired twice. One bullet passed through Slater's body from left to right and the other struck him in the leg. "Slater, however, had his nerve and made a quick shot at Woodrum, who fell dead." Ginn ran and was shot by Woodrum's companion, a man believed named Lykens.

Slater, who was found on the mountain by a search party after he had fired a signal, was taken by train to a Charleston hospital. A passenger on the train, who later reported the incident to a member of Woodrum's family, overheard Slater talking with the doctor who accompanied him. The doctor asked Slater where he had gotten all the scratches. Slater replied they came from a fight with Woodrum, that when Woodrum looked up over the sheltered cliff where Slater had fallen, Slater was waiting for him. He shot Woodrum, then fell over the cliff beside him. The two then fought like cats and dogs. All of a sudden Woodrum quit his scratching around and so did Slater. Woodrum started praying and Slater claimed he never heard a man in his life pray like that man did. The doctor then told Slater he doubted that Slater would make it to the Kanawha Valley hospital and that

Cleve Woodrum's grave at Eskdale in August 1978. PHOTO BY LOIS C. McLEAN

he had better be praying. Slater died in the operating room about four hours later.

A week after Woodrum's death, newspapers announced that a settlement had been reached on Cabin Creek. The settlement later proved unsatisfactory in many respects but one, and that was the removal of the Baldwin-Felts guards from Paint and Cabin creeks. Perhaps only those who suffered and finally rebelled against the mine guard system could appreciate the effort it had taken to be rid of the system. For Cesco Estep and Cleve Woodrum, who did not live to enjoy the new freedom, those who survived showed their appreciation by placing the small monuments over their graves.

Laura Woodrum later married Erwin Woodrum, and on Decoration Day each year until his death in 1947 the two visited Cleve Woodrum's grave. Until poor health prevented her, Laura Woodrum continued her visits. She died in Beckley in 1959.

Like Estep's children, Woodrum's moved off the creek and seldom returned. In May 1978 Ivory Woodrum Bayless was told her father's grave had been moved and coal trucks had made a path through the cemetery. Although in poor health, Ivory Bayless with her husband Hubert came to Eskdale where they found Cleve Woodrum's grave covered with rubble from the burned-out building. After removing the rubble, Ivory Bayless saw the unusual marker for the first time. She had left the area in the early 1920's

and did not recall its being there then. Her sister Grace Woodrum Huffman left the state because of her husband's black lung and mine injuries. She has never seen the marker either.

Woodrum's other children, except for Kenneth whose whereabouts are unknown to the author, are dead. Since meeting with the author at Eskdale in May 1978, Ivory Bayless has suffered a stroke which left her partially paralyzed and speechless.

The author first saw Cleve Woodrum's marker in December 1971 while on a research trip to Cabin Creek. The tour guide, Mr. Arnold Miller from Ohley, pointed out its location. In the spring of 1975 a student from West Virginia Institute of Technology, who had stumbled over Cesco Estep's marker, directed the author to its location. After interviewing members of the Estep family, the reason Estep's children could not find his marker became apparent. It had been put in the wrong place. With permission from the families, the marker was relocated over Cesco's grave. A memorial service and re-dedication of the monument, sponsored by the West Virginia Labor History Association, was held on the Sunday before Labor Day in 1975. For Clifford A. Estep, who had felt rather bitterly the loss of his father and the lack of appreciation for his sacrifice, that day was the happiest day in his life. Clifford died in November 1977, and his sister Frances F. Evans died in May 1978.

Although the presence of Estep's marker was hidden for years in the underbrush, Woodrum's was known to residents of Eskdale for over 50 years. Today, however, apparently no one knows who was responsible for purchasing and placing the monuments or when they were dedicated. Perhaps even more unfortunate is the fact that these men and monuments are unknown to today's members of the United Mine Workers of America, an organization whose members, at one time, appreciated their sacrifices enough to dedicate monuments to their memory.

The *West Virginia state motto struck an ironic note among union miners. This 1921 cartoon from the* United Mine Workers Journal *suggested mountaineers were anything but free.* COURTESY UMWJ

Walter Seacrist

A Songwriting Miner Remembers the Mine Wars

■ By Gordon L. Swartz III

Walter Seacrist was born on Paint Creek a few years before the big labor troubles broke out. Although too young to take part himself, he came from a union family and grew up with no doubts as to the right and wrong in labor-management affairs. The 1912–13 events left a lifelong impression, and Seacrist went on to become a strong union man himself. He affiliated with the radical branch of the miners' movement and participated in the final push toward unionization in the early 1930's. Walter Seacrist was a singing activist, writing many songs dealing with events of his childhood and later episodes of the Mine Wars.

This article by his great-nephew, also a union miner, was published in summer 1985.

My great-uncle, Walter Alexander Seacrist, was born Aug. 19, 1906, one of 12 children of William Henry and Lydia Johnson Seacrist. He was raised in the infamous coal camp called Holly Grove on Paint Creek in Kanawha County. He was just a youngster at the time of the 1912-13 labor troubles there, but he had strong memories of the period and later wrote songs about it. One was "Harrison County Jail," about his Uncle John's 99-year jail sentence (later revoked) for his part in the strike.

The first stanza expresses the viewpoint of a man bitter about being locked away without benefit of a civilian trial:

> Come all you jolly citizens
> And listen to my tale
> I'll tell you of a boarding house
> They call the county jail
> And if you don't believe me
> And think I'm telling a lie,
> Just come before some tinhorn court,
> You'll see the same as I.

Much later, Water elaborated on the story in taped recollections for my brother. "This song, 'Harrison County Jail,' of course, is about John," he reported. "Back in the '12 and '13 strike they had killed one of the Baldwin-Felts guards up at Gallagher, it is now—it was Mucklow then, the name of the place. They brought him out to Pratt and the state militia were stationed there. Martial law was in effect. There was one company of 'em stationed at Pratt and another stationed on the scale yard between Holly Grove and Gallagher. At Pratt the chief officer was Major James Davis.

"John, on the box that this guard's body was in, wrote with a piece of chalk: 'Another SOB gone to hell.' This Major Davis arrested him and John hit him. So they tried him in what we called the 'tinhorn court' there in the Pratt railroad depot. That was their guard house. And they sent him to the Harrison County jail. His sentence was 99 years."

The 'tinhorn court' was the military court at Pratt, for which Governor Hatfield later threw out the questionable sentences. Walter Seacrist believed that Mother Jones had a hand in the governor's decision, at least in the case of his uncle John. "Mother Jones went to the governor that had just been elected, Dr. Henry Hatfield, and got a pardon for him and went and brought him home," Walter concluded.

He reported other bloodshed, including the killing of another mine guard. This was "the night of the shooting at the station there at Holly Grove when the Baldwin-Felts guard was killed. His name was Stringer. Another one was shot, but he got in the weeds and crawled away and got to Hansford to the hospital and got away."

Walter said that his uncle was sought in that case as well. "There was something like 500 miners in Holly Grove that night, but the next morning they came to arrest John," he reported. "The girl, Gladys Perry, lived across the hollow, round back of the cemetery. She saw 'em coming and knew that they were after John and she came running around to tell him, fell over a rail fence, and broke her arm. But she got there and got him told before they got there, and he hid in the attic of Grandma Seacrist's house. They didn't get him.

"About the woman that was shot, Mrs. John Hall. She was having a baby at the time the Bull Moose train ran. She was shot in the foot the same night and from the same train Cesco Estep was killed." Of Estep's death, Walter went on, "I have a song about that. The title of it is 'Striker's Orphaned Child.' And it goes like this:

My father was a striker back in
  nineteen and thirteen.
He was the sweetest daddy; he never
  treated us mean.
He worked in dark and danger,
  almost day and night
To earn for us a living, to
  bring us all up right.

Walter sang several more stanzas into the tape recorder, bringing the ballad around to Estep's death while trying to get his family to safety and concluding with an assurance that they would all be reunited in the hereafter. "This was dedicated to Clifford Estep, whose father was killed from the Bull Moose train," he noted.

Like many miners, Walter Seacrist identified the chief villains of this period of the coal wars as Kanawha County Sheriff Bonner Hill and Governor William E. Glasscock. He seems to have taken a kinder view of Governor Hatfield, although he was not satisfied with Hatfield's eventual settlement of the strike. "Shortly after this," he said, "they had an election and Dr. Henry Hatfield was elected governor of West Virginia. He came up with what was known there in the coalfields as the Hatfield Agreement, broke the strike and put the miners back to work. And that's pretty much the story of the 1912-13 strike."

Walter himself got through the early bloodshed unscathed, but he had his troubles growing up. He contracted tuberculosis as a teenager and lay in bed for over a year. It was thought that he might never recover. When he did recover enough to get around, he was sent away from Paint Creek to live in Jackson County. He lived on a farm with a couple by the name of Meadows. The fresh air of Jackson County and the kindness of the Meadows family helped Walter in his slow recovery. Later he began working in the mines on Paint Creek, as had his father and brothers. He began preaching in the Baptist Church at age 19.

Walter, two of his brothers, and his father were working on a shift when the father was injured. Henry Seacrist was driving a car of coal out of the mine when the mule's back hit a sag in the roof. The mule panicked and lurched forward, dragging Walter's father up on the load of coal which he was hauling. His body went between the sagging roof and the load of coal. There was hardly any space there. It was said there couldn't have been over 14 inches of clearance.

Henry was taken to the hospital and expected to die. One eyeball had been pushed out of its socket. His ribs were crushed. He had multiple fractures and contusions. Against the odds, he lived, but his hair turned white during his week in the hospital. He was unable to return to work in the mine. Walter did not work in the mine for much longer himself. His father's accident left a terrible impression on him, as shown in his poem, "Blood on the Coal." It concluded by warning faraway consumers of the terrible price often paid for the fuel they took for granted:

Seacrist was born here in 1906. This later view shows younger sister Lois (left), and niece and nephew Georgia and Gordon Swartz. Gordon is the father of our writer, Gordon Swartz III. Date and photographer unknown.

You who live in cities, or out
  on the farm,
You don't know the thing
  called trouble,
You really don't know harm.
Firemen as you feed the furnace
To make the engine go,
Do you know there is some
  miner's blood
On all the coal you throw?

During 1931, Walter affiliated himself with the West Virginia Mine Workers Union, a dissident offshoot of the main United Mine Workers of America. John L. Lewis's United Mine Workers was having trouble in other quarters, and the miners of West Virginia felt abandoned. There was

much infighting among the hierarchy of the UMW. A large part of the West Virginia coalfields were striking and had to have some sort of an organization. Conditions at the mines and the coal camps did not allow the postponement of a strike until the UMW was ready to help.

Frank Keeney and Fred Mooney, two of the early UMW leaders in the southern coalfields, organized the splinter union in West Virginia. Among those rebels there was no love lost for John L. Lewis, as is evidenced by Walter's poem, "The Coal Miner's Dream." This is a dissatisfied miner's imagining of Judgment Day, when Lewis is found lacking as a union man— "and, by good St. Peter, was kicked down the golden stair!"

Governors Glasscock and Conley, as well as Sheriff Hill, quickly follow the UMW president down those stairs, but dissident leader Frank Keeney got a far kinder reception:

Next came Frank Keeney, a man
  they all knew well.
With a West Virginia Mine
  Worker's Agreement
He'd followed the operators to hell.
Then grand old St. Peter looked down
  the golden stair
And told him to come up higher
It was too hot for a union man
  down there.

Walter put his feelings as a preacher as

well as a unionist into this and other songs and poems, freely mixing religious imagery and strong labor sentiments.

A man now, in his late 20's, Walter was in on the concluding chapter of the struggle that finally brought full unionization to West Virginia's coalfields in the 1930's. These victorious years were less violent than had been the Mine Wars of his youth, but they were not without controversy. Brookwood Labor College of Katonah, New York, had representatives in the Kanawha Coalfields, and there were several other groups from outside the state also. These "agitators" were denounced by some in West Virginia, the word Bolshevik being used frequently. The press tried to foment a panic against the red menace. It is true that Brookwood was a socialist institution, but at the same time anyone who joined a union was considered a socialist by many. Coal operators portrayed themselves as trying to pro-

tect the state against the evil being taught by these "foreigners" from New York.

As usual, Walter Seacrist came to his own independent conclusions. Tom Tippett, a Brookwood professor, made his acquaintance during this period. Tippett was impressed with the young preacher-miner, and the two men became friends. Walter made trips to the Brookwood campus, taking classes and telling the Brookwooders of the plight of the coal miners. He also wrote "Tom Tippett" about his good friend:

There was a man in New York State
Tom Tippett was his name
To help the poor hard working man
To West Virginia came.

Several verses told of Tippett's work with Keeney and the miners, ending with the promise that the unionizing professor would be "coming back again."

The early 1930's brought Walter this new friend, and also farewell to an old one. Mother Jones died in 1930. Walter remembered her from as early as the Paint Creek-Cabin Creek strike. "I knew her, carried her little briefcase around for her in the big strike," he remembered of those childhood days. "I knew her again in the 1920-21 Logan County march." Not surprisingly, he participated in later memorial services at her grave.

"I was elected in 1932 to conduct the memorial services at her grave," he recalled in his taped recollections. "She died in Washington in early '30 and is buried in Mount Olive Cemetery in Mount Olive, Illinois. That's just a few miles out of Springfield. There at her grave there were just two stones. The headstone said 'Mother.' The footstone said 'Mother Jones.'

"I spoke there at this service at her tomb. Also the governor [actually U.S. Senator] of

An aging Walter Seacrist visits with his brother Clinton, a few years before his death in 1975. Photographer unknown, about 1970.

Walter and Virgie Seacrist in a quiet moment at home. Photographer unknown, 1965.

West Virginia, whose name was Rush Holt, was with me, and he also spoke. We spoke to some 60,000 miners and their wives that day." Walter concluded his taped reminiscences of the event by singing his version of "The Death of Mother Jones":

The world today's in mourning
For the death of Mother Jones
Gloom and sorrow hover
Around the miners' homes.

The origins of this old song are uncertain, but in his book *Only A Miner* folklorist Archie Green says Walter probably learned it from his friend Tom Tippett. Walter was proud of his version but did not seek credit for the song, as several others had done.

Nor did Walter Seacrist choose to work out the rest of his days as a West Virginia coal miner. He was disturbed by his father's fate and perhaps by coalfields warfare as well, or maybe as a union man he was

simply satisfied by the gains made in the 1930's. At any rate, he chose to move away and he finished his working life as a custodian at Cape Canaveral, Florida. It was there that he recorded these recollections, before his death of natural causes in August, 1975.

ANOTHER SONG BY WALTER SEACRIST

Of the many songs and poems left by Walter Seacrist, the most touching is "Law in the West Virginia Hills." Perhaps this is because it concerns a tragedy that, of all the tragic events of the unionizing period, came closest to his own heart. During the strike of 1930-31, the wife of Walter's imprisoned brother witnessed the eviction of Mrs. Chris Deviti from her company-owned house at Hugheston, Kanawha County. The company guards kicked the pregnant Mrs. Deviti in the stomach. Mrs. Seacrist, also pregnant, was untouched but deeply affected by the sight. She and her unborn child died mysteriously a few days later.

The song is sung to the tune of "The Little Rosewood Casket."

In a little village graveyard
Underneath a grassy mound
There sleeps a lovely maiden
In the cold and silent ground.

She was so tender-hearted,
So kind and noble, too.
People that knew her loved her.
If you could have met her, so would you.

She was young and hopeful.
She was full of youthful life.
She made our home more cheerful
She was my brother's wife.

My mother how she loved her,
As much as she loved her son.
She was so kind and cheerful,
It seemed her life had just begun.

My brother was a miner,
Toiling almost day and night,
Deep down in the coal mines
Away from God's sunlight.

To this valley came a union.
Brother joined with the band
To better his conditions.
Children were starving on every hand.

Then the cruel mine foreman,
To which my brother hired,
Learned he had joined the union,
Then he was quickly fired.

Then all over Kanawha Valley,
"We will strike," the miners said,
"For we are tired and hungry
And our children cry for bread."

These miners got together
One warm July day.
They laid away their tools
And struck for better pay.

Then the cruel company gunmen
With officers from all around
Came and drove them from
    their houses,
Threw their stuff out on the ground.

My sister saw these cruelties
As they terrorized the town.
She saw them murder unborn babies,
Kick these helpless mothers down.

Such cruel sights paralyzed her.
Something snapped in her head.
Not another word she uttered.
Two days later she was dead.

In Chillicothe prison
So very very far away
From his home and his loved ones
Brother sits and grieves today.

He was sent to this prison,
Whiskey was the charge they say,
By the law that cruelly murdered
His lovely wife that sad day.

Peace a stranger in the valley
Because justice is never there.
As you read this sad poem,
Tell me, do you think it fair?

My brother he is in prison,
His lovely wife she is dead,
While still in this same valley
Little children cry for bread.

Part III

The Logan-Mingo Wars, 1919–21

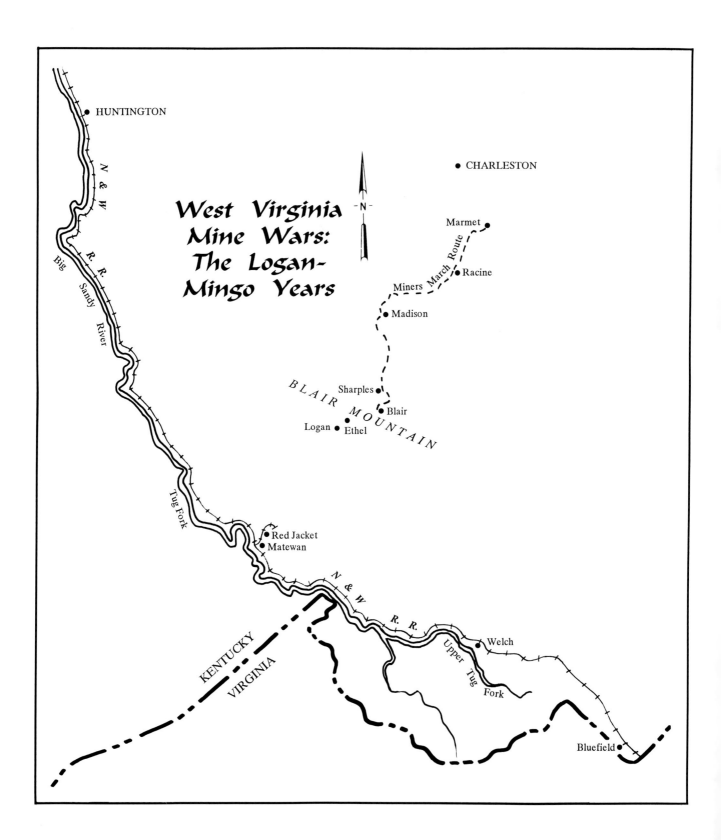

West Virginia
Mine Wars:
The Logan-
Mingo Years

"I'll Teach You Not to be Afraid"

Monia Baumgartner Remembers Mother Jones

■ By Lois C. McLean

After the bloody turmoil on Paint Creek and Cabin Creek, the coal industry settled into an uneasy truce for the duration of World War I. Ironically, the world peace that followed soon brought a renewal of labor warfare in West Virginia. As the international coal market soured, operators sought to offset falling prices by taking back some of labor's wartime gains. A resumption of hostilities was predictable, coming this time in West Virginia's youngest and southernmost coalfields, centering around Logan and Mingo counties.

The aging but indefatigable Mother Jones returned to take part in the Logan-Mingo war, her last major crusade in West Virginia. Countless Mountaineers remember Mother from this era, including Monia Foutch Baumgartner, interviewed by Lois McLean for the January–March 1980 GOLDENSEAL.

In 1919, Mother Jones and members of District 17, UMWA, began an organizing drive among the miners of Mingo County. According to Howard B. Lee, author of *Bloodletting in Appalachia*, Mingo County was known as "Bloody Mingo" because of the many blood feuds among its inhabitants, the most famous being that of the Hatfields and McCoys. With the coming of the Norfolk & Western Railroad and the developing coal industry, the feuds were replaced by labor wars. The United Mine Workers of America, which had a brief foothold in the area at the turn of the century, was determined, in 1919, to bring industrial democracy to Mingo County.

As usual, the tough, fearless old Mother Jones was a willing crusader for the miners' cause. Mother's Mingo County exploits are remembered by her few compatriots surviving from the time. Living quietly in Beckley with her two daughters is one woman whose experiences in those days are as vivid as they were 60 years ago. She is 89-year-old Monia Foutch Baumgartner.

Mrs. Baumgartner was born in Harlan County, Kentucky, on July 29, 1890. When she was 13 years old, Monia, her parents, four sisters, and three brothers moved to

West Virginia. Her father, Bill Foutch, had taken a trip to West Virginia and decided he liked it there. Returning home, he told his family to pack up. They were moving to West Virginia. The family settled on Pigeon Creek in Mingo County, where Foutch, a carpenter, found work building houses for the Island Creek Coal Company.

According to Mrs. Baumgartner, Devil Anse Hatfield and members of his clan were neighbors and "many, many a time" old Devil Anse came to their home. He and Bill Foutch often went hunting together. She recalled one occasion when they killed a bear. After dragging their kill home, Devil Anse asked Monia to make him some "willow" tea. Following his instructions, she went out and stripped some bark off a willow and a peach tree. With these, a third ingredient which she couldn't remember, and boiling water, Monia made the first of many pots for Devil Anse.

Cap Hatfield also lived nearby, but Mrs. Baumgartner's memories of him weren't as pleasant as those of his father. Once Cap Hatfield reportedly asked the local grocer to get him some cranberries. When the cranberries came, Mr. Adams, the grocer, forgot about Cap's order and sold the ber-

ries to his other customers. When the oversight was called to his attention, Mr. Adams was quoted as having said that Cap probably didn't know how to fix them anyway. Word got back to Cap and he came to the grocery store. When Mr. Adams saw him come in, he stuck out his hand and started to apologize. According to Mrs. Baumgartner, who was in the store at the time, Cap didn't wait to hear the apology but proceeded to lift Adams over the counter and to "beat him to a pulp." After wreaking his revenge on the hapless Adams, Cap said, "That's how I fix cranberries," and left the store.

Tennis Hatfield, another of Devil Anse's sons, Monia remembered as a soft-spoken and mild man unless he was crossed. But Sid Hatfield, a relative who was the chief of police in Matewan before being killed on the steps of the Welch courthouse by Baldwin-Felts "thugs," was not like most of the Hatfields. He was friendly and told jokes. He'd take a glass of whiskey but he wouldn't get drunk. He could handle whiskey, it didn't handle him. He was good-looking and had a pretty wife.

Married at 16 to a miner, "who was mean as a snake," Mrs. Baumgartner left him after

"I told her, 'Now listen here, Sister Jones, I'm afraid of bullets and snakes!' Mrs. Jones got tickled and laughed, but she was good to me."
PHOTO BY LOIS C. McLEAN

the birth of their third child. She worked in, and later operated boarding houses for miners to support herself and her children. It was during this period that she was recruited by Mother Jones.

Mrs. Baumgartner recalls, "I first met Mother Jones at my cousin's home. There was a miners' meeting going on and Mother Jones was there. I was sitting on the front porch when Mrs. Jones came out. She looked at me and then walked up to me. She asked me my name and I told her. She asked me where I was from and I told her Pigeon Creek. She asked me what my father did and I told her he was a carpenter. Then she asked me how old I was and I told her I wasn't so old, but old enough. Then she looked at me closer and said: 'I'd like to have you go with me sometime.' I told her: 'Oh, Mrs. Jones. I can't go with you. You and me couldn't get along. You ain't afraid and I am.' She said: 'I'll teach you not to be afraid.' But I said: 'I'm afraid Mrs. Jones, I couldn't go.'

"One day after that, she came driving up to our home in a little one-horse wagon. She stopped and called. 'Come with me. I'm just going to make a little talk. We won't be gone long.' I asked her: 'Now there ain't going to be any danger, is there Mrs. Jones?' 'Not much,' she answered.

"I went into the house and told my mother I was going with her and my mother

said I'd better not go. It was dangerous to be with Mother Jones and I might get killed. But I went on and got in the wagon. You know that little horse pulling the wagon was the prettiest and fattest one I had ever seen. And it minded her just like a baby or just like a child."

When asked how Mother Jones looked, Mrs. Baumgartner replied, "Why, do you know what she had from the skirt down? She was wearing a pair of men's overall pants! And a man's shirt! Yes, and some funny looking boots. They were sort of wool, men's kind, and they came up high, like they'd protect her if she fell. She had a man's hat, too, pulled down on her head.

"When we got to the hollow, I noticed a lot of men alongside the road and I wondered what in the world was Mrs. Jones going to do here. Then she stopped the wagon and told me to get out. She got out and reached under the wagon seat and pulled out a great big club, made like a ball bat, but not so long. I asked her what she was going to do with that. She said that I ought to have sense enough to know what she'd do with that if someone bothered her or me.

"Well we walked into those woods and there were a whole lot of men standing around," Mrs. Baumgartner recalls. "Mrs. Jones climbed up on a stump and she reached down and got a hold of my hand and told me to step up on the rock alongside the stump. Then she went to talking and I never heard such talking in all my life. Brother, she cussed like a drunk man. She said, 'You lowdown rascals you. You know what's good for you and what's bad for you. You looks bad to me already.' You see, she was trying to organize the union. She'd say anything. Told them she'd bet they didn't have no breakfast and half of them didn't have no home to live in. That they'd better get someone in there that would do something for them so as they could live neat. Then all at once, KA-WHOOM! A bullet went right between our heads and I'm a-telling you that liked to scare me to death. I said 'Now listen here, old woman, I'm getting out of here.'"

When asked what Mother Jones did, Mrs. Baumgartner replied, "She didn't do anything. Never a blink. She never paid a bit more attention than nothing. No, not a bit. She just said, 'Well, you can shoot again,

you _____. You missed me that time.' At that the men got tickled and they got to laughing. Mother Jones said they were laughing 'cause the bullet didn't hit her between the eyes. I told her, 'Sister, you're gonna be left alone if you don't hurry up and come go with me!' I was just about ready to start out of that hollow and she seen I was scared. I told her 'Mrs. Jones, you'd better hurry up now. You're gonna be left by yourself. I don't want to leave you and I won't. But I want you to hurry up and come on and go.'

"Then she turned to those men and said, 'You dirty lowdown _____s, you. You know! You know what you're doing. You're rotten. You're lowdown. You go home tonight and sit down with your children and your wife. Sit down and take your pencil and clear paper and *write*. Just write how you're living and what you've got. And just let the world know how you're living, and what you could have if you'd do the right thing.' Then she jumped off that stump and said, 'That's my farewell word to you, but I'll tell you one thing, I'll get you in the end.'

"We walked out of there and she never looked back. When we were in the wagon, she told me: 'Now don't you get scared. Just don't say too much about what was said or nothing. We'll be alright.' When we got to my house, Mrs. Jones came in and stayed awhile. But pretty soon, I could see she was thinking about something and she said she'd better get on. There was something she wanted to check on and believed she could make it on home. She got up, hugged and kissed me and said, 'Now I am going to come and get you again.' I told her, 'Yes, you will—if you can catch me.'"

Mother Jones did come back to visit young Monia several times, but she was never able to get her to attend another meeting. Each visit, it seems, was a memorable one for Mrs. Baumgartner. She told me of the time when Mrs. Jones and she were walking in the woods when she spotted a big snake "nearly two yards long," ahead of her. She remembers that she said "'Mrs. Jones, look there. Look at that big snake. Come on, let's get away from here.' But Mrs. Jones walked on past it like she didn't even see it and said, 'Good Lord, girl, if you aren't afraid of a bullet, you needn't be afraid of a snake.' I told her, 'Now listen here, Sister

Mother Jones looks decidedly more ladylike in this portrait than Monia Baumgartner recalls her as being.
PAINTING COURTESY JOSEPH OZANIC COLLECTION, WVU

Mother Jones in Mingo County. Left to right: Charley Workman, Red Doyle, Mother Jones, Warren Hutchinson, Sid Hatfield, Andrew Wilson, Ezra Fry, and Dave Phillips. Hatfield, police chief at Matewan, was later assassinated on the McDowell County Courthouse steps by Baldwin-Felts gun thugs. Photographer unknown, 1920. COURTESY WEST VIRGINIA COLLECTION, WVU

Jones, I'm afraid of bullets and snakes.' Mrs. Jones got tickled at me and laughed, but she was good to me."

Usually, when Mother Jones visited she only stayed for a few hours, but one time she did spend the night in Mrs. Baumgartner's boarding house. She recalls that Mother Jones acted like she wanted to sleep on the floor, in with the other boarders. Mother just asked her to make a pallet near the fire. Mrs. Baumgartner said no, Mrs. Jones should sleep upstairs in a room. Mother Jones replied, "Well, it might be alright if I sleep in a bed once in a while."

When asked if Mother Jones washed, changed clothes, or helped with the cooking when she stayed overnight, Mrs. Baumgartner remembered, "No, she didn't change clothes. She just pulled off those old britches and slept in the men's buttonhole pajamas she had on underneath them. I asked her if she wanted a pan of hot water to wash

in and she said, "Why do I want to wash? I'd wash and just have to turn around, scratch, and have to wash again." As for helping with the cooking, Mrs Baumgartner firmly replied, "No, ma'am. Lord have mercy, no! She was dirty. Why, I wouldn't eat a bite that she cooked under no consideration. Nor my mother wouldn't either.

"But she was good to me and I was good to her. Yes, I was. I had to be, 'cause, well, I was afraid not to be good to her. To tell you the truth, she really acted like she didn't care for anything. What she said, what she done, or what she wore. She didn't care nothing and if she had anything to say to you, she'd come right out and say it like it was. Now, some of the miners didn't like her. They were afraid she'd jerk and shoot their brains out. But they didn't talk sassy to her, no sir, 'cause the men were scared of her. They were afraid she'd jerk a gun and shoot their brains out. But they didn't talk

sassy to her, no sir, 'cause the men were scared of her. Well, I know I was scared of her and there ain't many people I'm scared of.

"But let me tell you. She made up with some people that was society, you know, that used good English. Law, you ought to heard her put out them big words. Yes, indeed. But if she was with someone her equal, she was just as mean as the devil, and she'd say or do anything to get you to laugh. She always liked a good laugh. She just never cared for nothing. You couldn't scare her. Why, one time when I told her she oughtn't to go someplace 'cause it was too dangerous, she said the miners were being treated dirty and she was going to help them. Then she laughed and said, 'You only die once.'"

When Mrs. Baumgartner finished talking about Mother Jones, she laughed, then shook her head, and said, "There just never was anyone like her."

The Gunfight at Matewan

An Anniversary Speech

■ By Lon K. Savage

The Logan-Mingo strike came to the boiling point on a dusty railroad siding at Matewan on May 19, 1920. Armed guards in the employ of the Baldwin-Felts Detective Agency came to town that day to evict striking miners from a nearby coal camp. On their way back through Matewan that afternoon they were accosted by strikers and strike sympathizers led by Matewan Police Chief Sid Hatfield and Mayor Cable Testerman.

The argument was brief and the ensuing gunfight even briefer, but the tragic results were long-lasting. Ten men were killed, mostly Baldwin-Felts "gun thugs," and the Mine Wars entered their final, bloody chapter. There was no peace in southern West Virginia for the next year and a half. Matewan took its place as the single most notorious event in the Mine Wars, the town's name becoming one of the catchwords of American labor history.

This article from the summer 1991 GOLDENSEAL is adapted from an anniversary speech delivered by Lon Savage at Matewan on May 19, 1989.

The Mingo County town of Matewan pauses each spring to remember the bloody massacre of May 19. The 1920 shootout between striking union miners led by Matewan police chief Sid Hatfield and Baldwin-Felts detective agents in the employ of the coal company was a turning point in West Virginia labor history. Hushed up for decades, the battle has been commemorated publicly in recent years as the people of Matewan and surrounding communities re-evaluate this part of their past. In 1989 they invited Lon Savage, author of the popular Mine Wars history, Thunder in the Mountains, to speak.

To me, Matewan is hallowed ground. Right here, Sid Hatfield and Mayor Testerman and the miners of Matewan faced off with the Baldwin-Felts detectives in one of the greatest gunfights in America's history.

And right over there by the river was the site of the little white church where the miners of Matewan signed up for the United Mine Workers in the spring of 1920, know-ing that it would cost them their jobs and in many cases their homes.

And over there, Anse Hatfield was killed in that summer of 1920.

And down at the other end of these buildings was where Mayor Testerman and later Sid Hatfield and Jessie, his wife, operated their store.

And down the river a piece was the Lick Creek tent colony, a fabulous place in those troubled times.

And that was near Williamson and the courthouse where Sid and more than 20 other Matewan boys were tried for murder of the Baldwin-Felts detectives in the winter and early spring of 1921, in what was then the biggest trial in West Virginia's history. They were found innocent because the jury apparently thought those Matewan boys did right when they killed the Baldwin-Felts detectives.

And all around Matewan the Three Days Battle was fought in the spring of 1921, a virtual reign of terror all along the Tug Valley.

And over there, where the depot stood, was where Sid and Jessie and Ed Chambers and his wife, Sallie, caught the train for Welch on that morning of August 1, 1921, for what turned out to be Sid and Ed's last trip.

And of course, across the river on top of that mountain is where Sid and Ed lie buried.

And if that isn't enough history for you, across the river is where the Hatfields tied three McCoys to a pawpaw bush and shot them dead. And all around here are memories of the old coal culture, coal camps, company towns, company houses, company stores, scrip, and all that.

These are things, people, and events of tremendous interest to all the people of America and, in fact, to people the world over.

That's why I have come to love this town of Matewan. It's a place of history, where people are known to stand up for what they believe in, a place where people have character. The Matewan area has more to brag

As an independent town surrounded by company-controlled territory, Matewan found itself in a precarious position. Miners used it as an organizing center, as shown in this union relief day scene. Photographer and date unknown. COURTESY STATE ARCHIVES

about than even it realizes. That's what I want to talk about.

Maybe the best way to talk about it is to compare what happened here with a similar event elsewhere. Do you remember the story of the shootout at the O.K. Corral?

If you're like me, you have some hazy recollection of it but don't remember the details. To refresh your memory, it was a famous gun battle in Tombstone, Arizona, in 1881. Wyatt Earp was the law enforcement official. He and his two brothers shot it out with five members of the Clanton gang in the O.K. Corral. Just about everyone is familiar with that famous movie scene, in which Wyatt Earp and his two brothers walk slowly, silently, three abreast, their guns in their holsters, down the streets of Tombstone to the O.K. Corral, where the five Clantons waited, guns ready to kill the Earps, as they've told everyone in town they would.

The suspense mounts as the Earps draw near the corral. People scatter and look down at the scene from upstairs windows. The Clantons reach for their guns, and everyone starts shooting. It was over in seconds. Wyatt Earp was in the thick of it, shooting from the hip in all directions. At the end, three of the Clanton gang were dead, and the other two fled, one bleeding. Both of Wyatt's brothers were wounded but not seriously. Wyatt stood triumphant.

That is a scene known throughout the world. It has been in movies, television, books, plays, dances, musicals, poems—in Europe, Asia and Africa. There aren't many places left in the world that that story hasn't reached. It has become a part of American mythology.

Yet, that story is no better than the story of what happened here at Matewan in 1920.

Sid Hatfield had a lot of the characteristics of Wyatt Earp—with Wild Bill Hickok, Jesse James, Billy the Kid, and Butch Cassidy and the Sundance Kid thrown in.

The drama preceding the shootout at Matewan was as great as at Tombstone, as the Baldwin-Felts detectives threw miners' families out of homes at gunpoint and the miners' fury rose to a boil.

They say 30 shots were fired at the O.K. Corral. At Matewan, more than 100 were fired.

Three men were killed in the O.K. Corral. At Matewan, ten were killed.

The similarities go on. After the shootout at the O.K. Corral, Wyatt Earp's enemies tried to get him in court on a murder charge, and when that failed they ambushed him and his brothers on two occasions, wounding one brother the first time, killing the other brother the second. Wyatt Earp survived.

After Matewan, Sid's enemies tried to get him, too, in the courts, with murder charges against him and the other Matewan boys. When that failed they ambushed him, shooting him and Ed Chambers on the courthouse steps at Welch in one of the most brutal slayings in our history.

The Matewan story has still more. During all of this, there was almost constant guerrilla warfare along the Tug Valley in 1920 and 1921, a time of terror. And after Sid's murder, 10,000 coal miners rose in rebellion, armed themselves, and marched across the state toward Mingo County to drive out the Baldwin-Felts detectives and everything they stood for. They fought the Battle of Blair Mountain in which tens of

Sid Hatfield, Jessie Testerman Hatfield and Cable Testerman were tragic figures at the center of the Matewan story. Taking Sid's side in the altercation with the Baldwin-Felts agents, Testerman was the first to fall in the shootout of May 19, 1920. Jessie, now widowed, married Hatfield within two weeks. She was widowed again the following summer when Sid was repeatedly shot while walking by her side up the Welch courthouse steps. Photographers unknown. SID HATFIELD PHOTO COURTESY STATE ARCHIVES, OTHERS COURTESY JACK TESTERMAN

thousands of shots were fired, planes dropped bombs, and 15 to 20 men were killed before President Harding sent in troops to restore order.

Tombstone can't match that. On balance, the O.K. Corral can't hold a candle to Matewan. Yet how Tombstone has capitalized on its history!

I recently talked with a woman who said she had grown up in Matewan, but she had never heard of the historic events that took place here until after she was married. When I came up through the public schools of West Virginia, like all the other kids I took periodic courses in West Virginia history. We learned about Indian mounds, Blenner-

hassett Island, how the state was formed in the Civil War, how the state capital was moved from one city to another, and about the contributions of the coal industry.

But in all those West Virginia history courses, I never heard of Sid Hatfield or the Matewan Massacre or the Battle of Blair Mountain.

It's ironic. We learned of Bacon's Rebellion in neighboring Virginia 300 years ago, and the Whiskey Rebellion in neighboring Pennsylvania 200 years ago, but we didn't learn of the miners' rebellion that our own parents took part in, right there where we were going to school—and the miners' rebellion may have been the largest of the three.

Apparently our historians and our parents were ashamed of that history. They were embarrassed. They weren't comfortable bringing up all that strife and bitterness again.

But you know, that history did happen. It happened right here in May 1920, and it spread to other parts of the region in the months afterward. It's part of a conflict that began before the turn of the 20th century, and that conflict continues to this day in the coalfields of Appalachia. It is a conflict that is as American as the Wild West. There is bitterness and strife in it, just as there always was and always will be in most important historic events.

The Battle of Matewan and the events that followed it in 1920 and 1921 constitute one of America's greatest stories and an important part of our history. The people in West Virginia and the Appalachian region are great, not despite these events but because of them. We should not be proud despite the events, we should be proud because of them. John Sayles, maker of the movie *Matewan,* recognized this when he said the story of Matewan and the events that followed is a story that "is as much a part of our heritage as that of the Alamo or Gettysburg or the winning of the West."

So let's treat it the way we treat the Alamo and Gettysburg and the winning of the West. Let's stop quarreling about who was right and who was wrong. There was enough right and wrong for everyone on both sides, just as there was at the Alamo and Gettysburg and the winning of the West—and at the O.K. Corral.

Let's tell everyone our history; let's brag about it; let's revel in it. Acknowledging and telling our history may even change the way we see ourselves. If the history of violence in Appalachian mining is ever to change, it will happen with an acknowledgment, a full airing, and an understanding of that history.

Now, at long last, it appears we are beginning to give our history the respect it deserves. Sayles's movie probably has done more than any other one thing in that regard. Denise Giardina's novel, *Storming Heaven,* based on events in Mingo County, has made the Book-of-the-Month Club lists. Historian David Corbin's work has shown us much about miners' lives in that troubled time. John Alexander Williams, one of West Virginia's foremost historians, has done much to tell about these forgotten events and to bring a needed balance to West Virginia's history. But there's a lot more to do.

Now, the town of Matewan, the states of Kentucky and West Virginia, the National Park Service and the Army Corps of Engineers are working together to develop a revitalization strategy for this area that includes increased recognition of the historic events which took place on this site and in this area. I say, more power to these people and to these efforts.

For the future, let the novelists, poets, movie makers, TV producers, dramatists, musicians, and historians come in and interpret our story, and reinterpret it and re-reinterpret it all they want and as they can. Let's do all we can, too, to preserve this rich history and to tell it to all who visit us or want to learn about us.

It will help Matewan. It will help West Virginia and this region. It will help the nation in better understanding us, as well as understanding its own history. It will improve the way others see us. Most important, it will help us understand ourselves and improve the way we see ourselves—the way we like ourselves. And that will change things for the better more rapidly than almost anything else we can do.

The shootout scene viewed from the east. The gunfire was concentrated toward the far end of the block of buildings at left.
COURTESY NORFOLK & WESTERN RAILWAY ARCHIVAL COLLECTION, VIRGINIA POLYTECHNIC INSTITUTE

Coalfields Vacations in the Mine Wars Era

■ By Harry M. Brawley

Suppose for a moment that this is the summer of 1918. A Charleston family is planning a vacation trip to the little Fayette County community of Cunard to visit their daughter. Would they be able to jump in a car and in about an hour and a half arrive at their destination? No such luck. In the first place, there probably would be no car, and if there was one, there were few paved roads outside of towns. It took the 1920 Good Roads Amendment to the West Virginia constitution to get our modern highway system off to a slow start.

My mother and I made such a trip to Cunard, where my sister's husband was the mine superintendent for the Coal Run Coal Company. These were troubled times in the coalfields, but the only difficulty we encountered lay simply in the travel arrangements.

First, we were driven in our pony-powered buggy to the Charleston C&O station to catch an early train. Hours later we reached Sewell. Then we took a horse and wagon for a bumpy ride down to the New River. There we transferred again, this time to a johnboat, to cross the river. Now the real fun began. My brother-in-law, T. S. Ray, met us with two horses, one for him and one for mother and me. The horses looked big compared to our ponies in Charleston, but we enjoyed the plodding ride up the side of the mountain to the coal camp.

Our hosts lived in a white house facing a gigantic lawn. There were horses, cows, and pigs running loose in the yard, and ducks and geese on a nearby creek. I was used to ponies and chickens at home, but I was intimidated by all the animals staring at me here. At first I wouldn't leave the big front porch, but finally got my nerve up and found many new friends among the calves and colts. Pigs were a complete mystery to me, although I soon learned to love the little ones.

Another curiosity was the company store, which intrigued me. It was a large barn-like building filled with everything from postage stamps to plows and stoves. This was my first contact with coal company scrip. I had always thought that money was coined only by the government, but I was wrong. Cus-tomers here made their purchases with metal discs issued by the company and good only at the company store.

On this trip I was introduced to the crank-type telephone. It rang incessantly, and it amazed me how our hosts knew when to answer their calls. Their party-line ring was two longs and a short, but since it was ringing all the time one had to pay attention. Everyone on the line could listen in, and if a caller talked too long he was roundly cussed out.

When our visit ended, we reversed our travel plan—horses off the mountain, john-boat across New River, the C&O to Charleston, and the pony cart home. What a vacation!

The next time we visited my sister and her husband he had a new job with the Raleigh-Wyoming Coal Company. He was superintendent of their operation at Ed-wight, a few miles above Whitesville in Coal River country. It is such an easy trip today—drive to Marmet, cross Lens Creek Mountain, and turn left on State Route 3. Follow that to Whitesville and on to Edwight. Simple? Not in 1920.

First, we took an interurban trolley from Charleston to Cabin Creek. Then we changed to a passenger coach on the end of a short freight train. We rode that way to Eskdale, where the car was switched to a train going to Whitesville. From there the car was backed into Edwight.

In 1922 my brother Jennings took a job with Raleigh-Wyoming as office manager for their large shaft mine at Glen Rogers in Wyoming County. He was there about 30 years, and I visited him often. The first time I went, I took the C&O from Charleston to Deep Water and then changed to a coach bound for Page. There we were shuffled around and coupled to a train going to Glen Daniel, and finally on to Glen Rogers.

This was a fair-sized town. The men were organized into three softball teams—the Grease Monkeys (tipple workers), the Rat Tails (underground miners), and the Cream Puffs (office workers). They played fast ball, and that made the job of the umpire very important. One day when the regular um-pire didn't show up, I was asked to substi-tute. I was a college boy at the time and fool-ish enough to accept. It was a raucous after-noon with lots of spirited arguments but no violence. No calls to "Kill the umpire!" even though my brother was a Cream Puff. But I was thankful when it began to rain, and we called off the game.

Glen Rogers was well organized with clubs and churches. There was a Boy Scout troop and my brother was scoutmaster. One of his scouts later became West Virginia's youngest governor up to that time. He was William C. Marland, who served from 1953 to 1957.

The small, largely non-denominational churches were an important part of life in the coalfields. Some were served by itinerant preachers, others shared pastors. If the church service was in the morning, Sunday School was in the afternoon, and vice versa, with a picnic at noon either way. Never before or since have I attended so many church picnics. The local church was a social as well as a religious center.

The ministers were by no means ignorant bumpkins. I heard a lot of interesting Bible interpretation from them. One old-timer was preaching on the story reported in the Acts of the Apostles where a sorcerer was trying to bargain with Saint Peter for the power to work miracles. The usual translation has Peter saying, "Thy silver perish with thee!" But the coalfields preacher said, "Can you imagine old rough Peter saying that? He more than likely said, 'You can take your money and go to Hell!'"

I have since reflected that although these were the climactic years of the violent Mine Wars in southern West Virginia, I recall no mention of labor troubles during my youth-ful visits with management families. No doubt the system was designed that way, to keep unpleasant realities from intruding on domestic life. It had the intended effect, in my case at least, for I found my biggest coal town adventures definitely in the getting there, threading my way through the net-work of roads and railroads of that long-ago era.

This was one movie where everyone stayed to see the credits. The atmosphere at Beckley's Crossroads Mall was festive—one person called it a "class reunion"—as cast and crew gathered for a special showing of the film *Matewan*, a fictional portrayal of the real labor struggles that led to Mingo County's 1920 "Matewan Massacre." As in the movie itself, West Virginians greatly outnumbered the out-of-staters in attendance.

Just before showtime, writer and director John Sayles made his appearance. Speaking of his experiences in making the film, which was shot entirely in West Virginia, he said, "it was just great. One of the best things about it was to hear the Matewan story back 100 times—it was good for the actors who didn't come from around here. People knew the stories but they're not taught in schools. A lot of labor history isn't taught in schools. "

The stories in question are those surrounding the attempt to organize the mines of the Tug Valley in the early 1920's. Union men and Matewan police chief Sid Hatfield confronted the industrial establishment, particularly "gun thugs" from the hated Baldwin-Felts Detective Agency. The film culminates in a climactic shoot-out which resulted in the deaths of seven thugs, including two of the Felts brothers, as well as two miners and Mayor Testerman of Matewan. That bloodbath came to be called the Matewan Massacre. It brought the retaliatory murder of Hatfield on the steps of the McDowell County courthouse and the famous 1921 Miner's March on Logan and Mingo.

The film opens up in the blackness of a coal mine, really Beckley's Exhibition Mine, where workers made whispered plans for a strike. As the strike progresses, the company imports blacks from the Deep South and Italian immigrants fresh off the boat to work as scabs. Union organizer Joe Kenehan, played by Chris Cooper, arrives to face the hostility of the company and the prejudices separating the diverse groups of miners.

Kenehan, now organizing for the United Mine Workers, is a former member of the Industrial Workers of the World. The "Wobblies," as IWW mem-

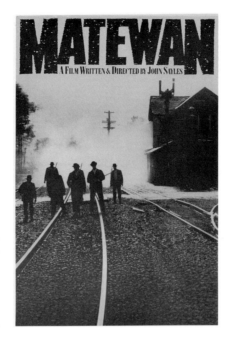

MOVIE REVIEW

bers were popularly known, were radical and courageous believers in the gospel of "One Big Union" to represent all working people, regardless of race, occupation or gender. Their organization was brutally repressed in the years following World War I. In the film, Kenehan was imprisoned during the war for his pacifist beliefs that the international conflict amounted only to "workers killing workers." In the coalfields his peaceful militancy contrasts effectively and tragically with prevailing violent emotions.

In large measure, *Matewan* is the story of how the miners overcome differences to stand together. In one powerful scene, the leader of the black miners, Few Clothes Johnson (superbly played by James Earl Jones) walks into a startled assembly of all white miners, saying "I got business with the union... . I been called a 'nigger' before. There ain't no helpin' that, being how white folks are. But I never been called no scab!" The Italians follow suit, and the miners and their families face hardships and evictions from company housing together. Sayles makes particularly effective use of folk music to make his point, as the melodies of Italian mandolins, black harmonicas, and hillbilly fiddles gradually harmonize.

Against this background, many sub-plots develop. Daniel, a teenaged preacher, grows to manhood in the struggle and departs from Baptist orthodoxy after seeing his best friend murdered by the mine guards. The strikers' solidarity is tested by company intrigues. And finally Sid Hatfield (David Strathairn), who watched in helpless rage while miners were evicted from company housing, draws the line in Matewan. A former miner, Hatfield's attitude is fiercely paternalistic, as expressed in lines like "I take care of my people. You bring'em trouble, you're a dead man." In one scene, Hatfield warns two mine guards that if either dares to "lift a finger in town limits, I'm gonna put you away."

As the historical record shows, fingers were indeed lifted and people were "put away." When the smoke clears, the unarmed Kenehan lies amid the carnage. The film ends with the voice of an aged miner—who turns out to be the grownup Daniel—musing over the course of events. He concludes, "It's just 'one big union, the whole world over,' Joe Kenehan used to say and from the day of the Matewan Massacre that's what I preached. That's my religion."

If the movie sounds unbearably grim, it is not. There are many occasions for the audience to laugh, as the characters display that genuine West Virginia trait of finding humor in the worst of situations. Indeed, the most striking thing about the entire film is its authenticity. Despite whatever inevitable liberties may have been taken with history, the story rings true. Those are our hills, our mines, our people. Traditionally, West Virginians have come off poorly in the media, and the Appalachian region has been exploited culturally as it has been economically. *Matewan* is a happy exception. It is a film we can take pride in.

One question remains. Were the Mine Wars a "blot in the state's history," as a correspondent for the *Washington Star* wrote in 1921, or were they West Virginia's finest hour, as the miners' grandchildren who helped in the making of *Matewan* believe? That depends on how you answer the question in the old miners' song, "Which Side Are You On?"

—RICK WILSON

See page 109 for ordering information.

The Dust Settles

Felts Papers Offer More on Matewan

■ By Topper Sherwood

Among the fallen at Matewan were Albert Felts and Lee Felts, brothers of Tom Felts, the managing owner of the Baldwin-Felts Detective Agency. Tom Felts was enraged personally and professionally, and he spared neither time nor expense in building a case against Hatfield and his allies. Recently discovered Felts papers reveal a remarkable undercover investigation, beginning the day after the shootout, as discussed in this article from the summer 1991 GOLDENSEAL.

"Dear Tom," the letter begins, "Except My sincear sympthey. I am sending you a List of names. The ones checked are Murders & The rest are witnesses. I would advise That They be arested & Put under Bond."

The letter is dated May 20, 1920 — one day after Thomas Felts's brothers, Albert and Lee, were gunned down by a group of angry men in Matewan, Mingo County. Tom Felts managed the Baldwin-Felts Detective Agency in Bluefield, hiring Lee, when he could be pulled away from his timber business, and working Albert full-time. The Felts agency, in turn, was employed by coal companies to insure—often by force—that the United Mine Workers union never gained the foothold it sought in southern West Virginia.

But now Tom Felts was engaged in more urgent business, the investigation of a bloody assault on the agency itself. On May 19, the two Felts brothers and ten guards had cleared five Stone Mountain Coal Company houses of miners who'd broken corporate policy by joining the union. After an early dinner at the Urias Hotel, the detectives were confronted by Matewan police chief Sid Hatfield and at least 20 other men in and around Tom Chambers's hardware store. The resulting shootout ended in the deaths of seven guards and three townspeople, including Matewan Mayor Cable Testerman.

The sympathy letter quoted above is part of the newly-surfaced Felts Collection—scores of memos, reports, and news clippings kept by Thomas Felts following the ambush in Matewan. The papers, discovered last year in a warehouse and acquired by the Eastern Regional Coal Archives in Bluefield, include what appear to be excerpts from the earliest reports of Felts's undercover detectives in the field. Furtively composed, the agents' original reports were signed with clandestine code names: "Operative No. 9," "Operative No. 31," and "Operative No. 19." The agents sent their detailed findings to a Bluefield post office box, maintained by the agency under a false name.

"It is generally being talked among the men here that Sid Hatfield shot and killed A. C. Felts and [detective] C. B. Cunningham," Operative No. 31 writes, in a filing dated May 23rd. "I have discussed the matter with several eye witnesses, all of whom seem to be of this belief."

"Reese Chambers and Sid Hatfield," says another report, "received credit for killing the majority of the Baldwin-Felts men."

Of the Baldwin-Felts agents, only the identity of "No. 9" is well-known today. Charlie Everett Lively, a trusted union member who doubled as a Baldwin-Felts employee for more than a decade, had moved into the region in January or February. After linking up with several union locals, he cleverly opened a restaurant in the same building where UMW organizing meetings were held. His Matewan eatery became a popular hangout for union members, allowing Lively to hear about the gunfight firsthand. During the next few months, the secret company agent held many conversations with the battle's surviving principals and eventual trial defendants—Sid Hatfield, Reece Chambers, Fred Burgraff, and others.

"Sid Hatfield said he was standing in the door right next to A. C. Felts when the shooting started," says one of Lively's reports, "but A. C. Williams, Raymond Chambers, Fred Burgrass [sic], and others say he was not."

Most of Felts's agents reveal their sources of information and, in cases of second-hand material, where those people allegedly had heard it. Taken together, the Felts documents offer a fascinating account of what was being said and heard by people in Matewan and Williamson following the shootings. The picture emerges of a sizeable network of spies extracting evidence from a provincial community whose anger and fear had driven some of its members to unparalleled violence.

Overshadowing the entire conflict that spring were the competing campaigns launched by the United Mine Workers and the Operators Association of Williamson Field. The coal association represented 56

Thomas L. Felts was a dangerous man, hated throughout the coalfields. He traveled widely from his Virginia home. Photographer and date unknown. COURTESY EASTERN REGIONAL COAL ARCHIVES

operations, whose owners had agreed to compel all their employees to sign "individual agreements." The agreements, dubbed "yellow-dog contracts" by miners, pledged laborers to remain nonunion and never to work near union members. In their new organizing effort, UMW activists decried the contracts—along with the presence of company police, the Baldwin-Felts guards.

With such volatile issues, the secrecy maintained by both sides, and the sheer number of people involved, solid information on the "Matewan Massacre" was hard to come by—even for those who lived there. Thomas Felts's agents sent many conflicting accounts of what actually happened on that drizzly day in May 1920. One report, dated June 11, offers Hatfield's version of the battle, told to the reporting agent by a mutual friend in Huntington: "Mr. Felts fired from his coat pocket, mortally wounding Tester-man, and then fired over his shoulder at Sid Hatfield, killing [Matewan resident] Tot Tinsley instantly. . . . At this time, Sid Hatfield opened fire, killing Albert Felts."

Tom Felts subsequently ordered the author of that report, Operative No. 19, to

spend more time in the area. Felts's goal was to build a case. "I want No. 19 to spend the next ten days or two weeks in the Matewan fields," he wrote, "in order to pick up all information he possibly can between this time and the time the grand jury meets, on June 21st." Some of the agents' reports echo a siege mentality, with at least one Felts correspondent suggesting that union sympathizers virtually controlled the entire area. Nonetheless, this man felt, "we will not find any one of the better class, either in Matewan or Williamson, accept [sic] those directly connected with Sheriff Blankenship or Sid Hatfield, who are in sympathy with them."

The town's volatility during the grand jury investigation worried Felts and his men.

"I am afraid that the important witnesses will be intimidated and probably killed," wrote one correspondent on June 27. "The witnesses who are afraid of their lives are as follows: Squire A. B. Hatfield, Ance [sic] Hatfield, Janie Mullins. Others are afraid to fully express the fact, due to having to leave town. I was advised by property owners that they were making efforts to dispose of their holdings in the town for fear

of being killed."

It was reported that Anse Hatfield, a Matewan hotel proprietor and not the Devil Anse of feud fame, had been threatened. Anse, who had testified against Sid before the grand jury, received a note, saying, "Arrange your business if you have any. You have not got long to live."

In this case, at least, the fears were well-founded. A few weeks later, Anse Hatfield was killed on the front porch of his Urias Hotel. Sid Hatfield was charged in connection with that shooting, in addition to the killings of May 19.

For all the new information they offer, the Felts papers are bound to raise as many questions as they resolve. The role of Isaac Brewer, for example, may deserve a closer look. "A man by the name of Deskins . . . said he saw Brewer go into the front of the [hardware] store and went back to the rear and shoved his pistol right over someone's shoulder against A. C. Felts' temple," says one memo.

Lively writes that witness Jesse Stafford told an agent that "Isaac Brewer called to Hatfield to come over to the hardware store, and A. C. [Felts] let him go, and then fol-

Part of Felts's challenge was to reconstruct the scene of the shootout, which claimed several employees, including two of his brothers. The above photo is a contemporary view of the area where much of the shooting happened, with the Matewan post office in the corner building. The Chambers hardware store is in the building at left. The trial model (below) shows these buildings at the near end of the historic block.

ABOVE PHOTO COURTESY N&W RAILWAY COLLECTION, VPI; MODEL PHOTO COURTESY STATE ARCHIVES

The shootout scene as it appears today, with the post office bricked up and a newer building in the old vacant lot.
PHOTO BY MICHAEL KELER

lowed him over there. Stafford also said just as the shooting started, Brewer told A. C., 'You have a warrant for the wrong man (meaning Sid Hatfield), you are not going to take him,' and then the shooting started."

Another memo says: "Dr. R. M. Music, of Williamson, owner of the Mingo Republican Paper, was in the office today and volunteered . . . that Isaac Brewer fired the first shot and that he evidently killed A. C. Felts."

Witnesses at the trial later placed Brewer in the store *between* Sid Hatfield and Albert Felts when the shooting started. Testimony also indicates that Brewer—who had drawn his gun and was wounded in the opening volley—faced the doorway that framed Felts and Testerman, giving him (along with Hatfield) an open shot at both.

Despite the evidence against him, though, charges against Brewer were dropped after he struck a deal with the prosecution and agreed to testify against Hatfield and the

rest.

Another ongoing question is the tangled relationship of Sid Hatfield, Sid's ally Cable Testerman, and Testerman's wife, Jessie. Three days after the shootings, one Felts correspondent reported that "the concensus [sic] of opinion among the citizens of Matewan is that Sid Hatfield shot Mayor Testerman himself, for the reason that he (Hatfield) is in love with Testerman's wife."

This issue became public a week or so later, when Hatfield and Jessie Testerman were discovered together in a Huntington hotel. The couple, who had purchased a marriage license that day, were wed after spending a night in jail on charges of "improper relations." Thomas Felts used the incident to publicly declare that "Hatfield shot Testerman to get him out of the way." Hatfield countered with his story that Albert Felts had killed Mayor Testerman with the first shot of the gunfight.

Other reports from the Felts papers offer

more information on the romance angle:

• "Old Aunt Jane Chafin, made the statement [that] there was a terrible lot of talk about Sid Hatfield and Mrs. Testerman, and it was believed Testerman knew all about it and sooner or later there would be a killing."

• "Tom Hatfield told Mr. Gates that on one occasion, sometime in the year 1917, Testerman's wife tried to get him to kill her husband."

• "Conductor Griffin says that Pullman Conductor _____ says that Mrs. Testerman made the statement to him on the train . . . that Sid Hatfield killed her husband."

Sometime after the court acquittal of the Matewan defendants—and after Lively and other Baldwin guards later gunned down Hatfield on the courthouse steps in Welch—the detective agency apparently produced a bitter account of Sid and Jessie's lives. Sid, "the Terror of the Tug," is taken to task for a history of violence, gambling, and bootlegging. In the "Record of Mrs. Sid Hatfield," Jessie is portrayed as "a lewd woman" from "a very young age" who had been "kept" by Testerman before he married her. The document says Testerman had quarreled with and "whipped" his wife the night before the battle, and that Jessie had "sent a note to Sid, in which she told him to watch her husband, the Mayor."

But, more substantially, a reading of the Felts papers shows the extent to which people in the southern coalfields were subject to a system of frontier justice. Felts's private detective agency held a great deal of authority in bringing the Matewan case to court, and apparently filled requests for information from Governor John Cornwell. Thus, with the unofficial nod from the highest levels of state government, Felts was able to go ahead with his investigation by private police force. He pursued the matter vigorously.

"I want to get Tyrec to look this man up immediately and . . . if necessary, have him arrested and interviewed," says one of his memos.

"A man named Moore . . . showed great prejudice against the detectives, and sympathy for the other side," says another. "Look up this man Moore."

And finally: "A. D. Dickey, cashier of the Matewan Bank . . . is believed to know a good deal about the shooting. . . . However, he would not [tell everything he knows] while he is under the present influences. Investigate Dickey and find out if he is married; how much salary he is getting at the Matewan Bank; if he is an efficient cashier and if he is a man worthy of a better job, and it might be he could be pulled away from there and given a job elsewhere, in which case he might tell all he knows."

Such correspondence underlines the remarkable power Felts commanded from his Bluefield office. Considering that he was

brother and employer of the victims, his influence in the prosecution—his apparent ability to subpoena, interrogate, and even relocate witnesses—contradicts modern ideas of blind, impartial justice.

The Felts papers further serve to remind us how intensely divisive the ambush and coal strike were. The memos and other documents portray Matewan as a rough-and-tumble town, thick with personal and political vendettas. At the same time, the detectives' reports, while remarkably cool in their approach, carry a quiet sense of vengeance of their own. The sides were clearly drawn.

Ultimately, the shooting likely will continue to be seen as an act of rebellion against industrial authority, vividly personified by the Baldwin-Felts guards. As one elderly Matewan resident put it: "I don't know how many [were killed]. . . . But I do know they'd have liked to kill 'em all."

The widows of Sid Hatfield and Ed Chambers outside the U.S. Senate. The two women traveled to Washington to testify before Senate hearings on coalfields violence in September 1921.
PHOTO BY HARRIS AND EWING, COURTESY WEST VIRGINIA AND REGIONAL HISTORY COLLECTION, WVU

Sid Hatfield's tomb stands vigil over the more peaceful Tug Fork country today. The mountains of West Virginia loom behind Hatfield's grave, which is on the Kentucky side of the river. PHOTO BY MICHAEL KELLER

A MATEWAN CHECKLIST

Those wanting to learn more about Matewan and the West Virginia Mine Wars should check the following recent works:

✔ *Life, Work, and Rebellion in the Coalfields: The Southern West Virginia Miners, 1880-1922*, by David Alan Corbin. (University of Illinois Press, $12.95 paperbound). This scholarly history treats the miners' rebellion in social context.

✔ *The West Virginia Mine Wars: An Anthology*, edited by David Alan Corbin (Appalachian Editions, $9.95 paperbound). A collection of excerpts from testimony, journalism and other primary documents of the Mine Wars era. The book includes first-hand accounts of Sid Hatfield, C. E. Lively and other key participants in the conflict.

✔ *Storming Heaven*, by Denise Giardina (Ivy Books/Random House, $3.95 paperbound). The Matewan story broadly fictionalized by a daughter of the coalfields. McDowell Countians will recognize the historic photo of Hemphill on the cover.

✔ *The Autobiography of Mother Jones*, by Mary Harris Jones (Charles H. Kerr, $12.95 paperbound). A highly readable if often embroidered account of the famous labor organizer's adventures in West Virginia and elsewhere.

✔ *Thunder in the Mountains: The West Virginia Mine Wars, 1920-21*, by Lon Savage (University of Pittsburgh Press, $9.95 paperbound). A very successful popular history by the author of our article.

✔ *Matewan*, a film by John Sayles (Red Dog Films). This movie shot on location in the Fayette County town of Thurmond played for weeks in coalfield theaters. There is graphic violence unsuitable for young children.

The above books may be found in public libraries or purchased in regional bookstores. The movie Matewan may be rented in a VHS video version.

The Red Neck War of 1921

The Miners' March and The Battle of Blair Mountain

■ By Michael M. Meador

The assassination of Matewan Massacre defendants Sid Hatfield and Ed Chambers in August 1921 brought the West Virginia Mine Wars to a frenzied crescendo. Outraged coal miners marched South from the Kanawha Valley by the thousands, determined to end the nonunion regime in Logan and Mingo. They were intercepted by Logan Sheriff Don Chafin, an infamous figure in union history. Chafin's men met the miners along a broad defensive front just inside the northern Logan border, and The Battle of Blair Mountain began. It took the U.S. Army to end it.

Michael Meador's articles on Blair Mountain were published in the April–June 1981 GOLDENSEAL. Russell Foglesong's reminiscences about Sheriff Chafin were published in fall 1989.

For six days the *Charleston Gazette*'s headlines screamed: "Troops are Ordered Here!," "Martial Law in Five Counties," "Troops Invade Boone County," "Hard Battle on Two Fronts of Logan Line." A war was in progress in West Virginia. As many as 15,000 men were involved, an unknown number were killed or wounded, bombs were dropped, trains were stolen, stores were plundered, a county was invaded and another was under siege. The president had to send in federal troops, the United Mine Workers of America was fighting for its life—and today, almost unbelievably, this war is nearly forgotten. There is not even a roadside marker to commemorate the mine war known variously as The Battle of Blair Mountain, the Miners' March, or the Red Neck War.

The general causes of the conflict of 1921 developed over many years. From the time the first shovelful of coal was removed in West Virginia, the men who did the mining were exploited by those who owned the mineral.

Miners and their families often existed in crowded, isolated, and substandard coal camps, at the mercy of the mine owners

who owned the camps as well. Miners who fought for better wages or living conditions were fired from their jobs, thrown out of their homes, and blackballed at other mines. One either accepted the system or moved on.

A ray of hope appeared for the miners in 1890 when the United Mine Workers of America was organized by a merger of two earlier miners' unions. By the turn of the century unionized mine operators in the northern and midwestern fields were putting pressure on the UMWA to organize the younger West Virginia industry, whose cheap coal was undercutting established markets.

Threatened with the loss of their foothold in these older coalfields, union officials set about trying to organize West Virginia. They were met with resistance by mine owners and the courts. Injunctions were issued against the use of coercion or violence to force miners to become union members. West Virginia mine owners hired special guards and deputies (called "thugs" by the miners) for the purpose of keeping the union out.

One of the most hated tools of the mine owners was the "yellow dog" contract which many miners were forced to sign. In the contract the miner agreed not to join the union under penalty of losing his job and company house. These contracts, upheld in court, were a powerful weapon in the hands of the operators and much resented by the miners.

In the early 1900's the majority of West Virginia's mines were owned and operated by individuals or a few investors, rather than large corporations. Many of these operations were tiny by today's standards, although they employed more workers than might be expected, since coal was mostly mined by hand labor. Owners of these mines found it difficult to absorb financial losses. They feared the union because of its insistence upon such costly practices as higher wages, safer working conditions, and collective bargaining.

In spite of this fear of unions, roughly half the mines in the state had accepted the UMWA by 1910. But most of these mines were north of the Kanawha River. South of the Kanawha the mine owners and their hated guards ruled. To assure complete control

Bill Blizzard at about the time of the Battle of Blair Mountain. Photographer unknown.
COURTESY LON SAVAGE

over their operations and to keep the union away, mine owners in West Virginia gradually gained control of local and state government through the use of coercion, vote buying, bribery and fear. The frustrated miners soon realized that no help for their grievances would come from courts or elected officials, and turned to use of strikes and violence to settle their disputes. This made their cause feared and unpopular with the general public.

In 1912 the first major strike in the West Virginia Mine Wars occurred on Paint and Cabin Creeks in Kanawha County, when 7,500 walked off the job over a wage dispute. The operators, refusing to negotiate, fired the miners and evicted them from their company-owned homes. Thousands of people were forced to take shelter in the woods and slopes above the two creeks.

Mother Jones, the fiery, foul-mouthed union organizer, arrived and encouraged the miners to take up arms. The union provided guns and ammunition, and for weeks the two creeks were a bloody battlefield. Only when the enraged miners seemed likely to wipe out the mine guards did the governor declare martial law and send in the state militia to end the strike. The violence, however, continued into the next year.

In 1917 America's entry into World War I brought a short truce to the continuing struggle between union and industry in the coalfields. The market for coal was good and most of the younger labor force was fighting overseas. But tension surfaced again as soon as the war ended. In 1919 an armed band of pro-union miners marched through Boone County in an attempt to organize the Logan and Mingo county mines. They were stopped at Danville in Boone County when word reached them from the governor to either disband peacefully or face the state militia. The march ended without incident.

On May 19, 1920, several mine guards (including Albert and Lee Felts of the notorious Baldwin-Felts Detective Agency), who had been evicting miners from company houses in Mingo County, were ambushed and slaughtered in downtown Matewan. The battle, led by Police Chief Sid Hatfield, also claimed the lives of Matewan's mayor and two miners. Hatfield and his henchmen were trumpeted as champions of the union cause and were acquitted for lack of evidence when brought to trial for the murders. The mine guards sought revenge, however, and Hatfield and an associate were gunned down in broad daylight on the steps of the McDowell County Courthouse the next summer.

All during that troubled summer of 1921 there was violence and unrest in the southern coalfields. Fighting got so bad in Mingo County that Governor Morgan declared martial law there.

To protest the murder of Hatfield and the conditions in Mingo County, the leaders of the union called for a rally at the state capitol on Sunday, August 7, 1921. Mother Jones was invited to speak to the group. She reviled the governor and coal companies in the foulest language and called upon the miners to march into Logan and Mingo counties and set up the union by force.

In Logan County this would mean crushing the power of Sheriff Don Chafin, who was paid by the coal companies to keep out the union. He sustained a force of 300 "special deputies" whose purpose was to watch all incoming roads and railroads and to prevent rallies at the mines. Suspicious characters were jailed without legal recourse and many persons, it was reported, simply disappeared. Don Chafin virtually ruled all aspects of life in Logan County and was hated and feared by the union.

At the capitol rally on the seventh, Mother Jones called for the miners to lynch Chafin and to establish the union at all costs. Frank Keeney, the UMW District 17 president, urged the miners to return to their homes, arm themselves, and wait for a call to action.

Mother Jones and Keeney were calling for the union to gamble its future in one desperate show of force. They realized that if the march was successful and the union could be carried by force into Mingo and Logan counties, the bastion of nonunion labor, then the UMWA would be free to organize any mine in the state.

However, they surely must also have realized that if the armed march was unsuccessful the union would probably be cast out of the southern West Virginia coalfields altogether. It would take years to recover from such a loss.

The call to arms came on August 20, 1921. On that day 600 armed men gathered at Lens Creek, near Marmet in Kanawha County. The area became an armed camp as angry men swarmed in from all parts of southern West Virginia and surrounding areas. Some reportedly came from as far away as Kentucky, Pennsylvania, and Ohio. A few men wore uniforms and helmets, left over from army service in World War I.

Union officials, such as Frank Keeney and Fred Mooney, publicly denied leadership of the mob. Newspaper reporters tried to determine the identity of the leaders but were unsuccessful. Observers reported that the miners organized themselves into small units and elected leaders of these groups, but no one seemed to be in charge of the whole assembly.

By the late afternoon of August 21, 1,500 men had gathered at Lens Creek. Their destination and purpose was kept a secret and reporters and law enforcement officers were turned away. The *Charleston Gazette* reported that the miners were rumored to be preparing to invade Logan County but no one in authority could be found to verify the rumors. Residents of Charleston were thrown into a panic by rumors that the miners, who were only 10 miles away, were going to attack the capital city.

By the 23rd the number of miners had swollen to between 7,000 and 8,000. Still no leaders emerged publicly. Flu and dysentery invaded the miners' unsanitary camp, and six doctors and eight nurses were brought in to care for the victims.

That night Mother Jones spoke to the assembled miners and, for reasons still unknown, reversed herself and urged the miners to disband and go home. She said she had received a telegram from President Harding ordering the men to disperse. The telegram was proven to be bogus and Mother Jones left the miners' camp discredited and in disgrace. The incident weakened her influence over the miners and she left West Virginia, to return only briefly a few years later.

In spite of Mother Jones, preparations for the invasion continued. Finally, on the night of August 24, somewhere between 8,000 and 13,000 men started up Lens Creek toward Logan, 65 miles away. When the news reached Logan early in the morning, shop whistles blew and church bells were rung in alarm. Sheriff Chafin rushed his deputies to the top of Blair Mountain to man the fortifications that had been thrown up in preparation. Also Chafin called out every able-bodied man available.

Don Chafin chose Blair Mountain as a line of defense because of several factors. The mountain effectively divides Logan County into two unequal parts, the larger of which is drained by the Guyandotte River which flows northwest towards Huntington. This southern area was Chafin's stronghold, was nonunion, and bordered Mingo County.

The smaller northern section was drained by the Little Coal River which flows northeast toward the Kanawha River at St. Albans. This smaller section of Logan County had union mines and bordered Boone County.

To reach Logan from Charleston, one either had to take the train to Huntington and then up the Guyandotte to Logan, travel by dirt road, or by train up the Coal River through Madison to the foot of Blair Mountain in Logan County, where the rails ended. From there one crossed the mountain by foot, wagon, or horse to Logan on the other side. The easiest route was through Huntington but the most direct was through Boone County and over Blair Mountain.

The marchers followed a winding, mountainous, dirt road from Marmet, which is the present-day route of U.S. 119 into Madison.

The Charleston Gazette telephoned Boone County Sheriff John L. Hill and asked him what he intended to do to stop the thousands of miners. The sheriff replied that he only had three or four deputies and as far as he was concerned the miners were "perfectly welcome to walk along the highway through Boone County."

A fast-moving advance group of miners reached the foot of Blair Mountain early on the morning of August 25. There they were surprised by a group of Chafin's men and a pitched battle broke out. The miners retreated.

In the meantime the main group of marchers was stretched out in a long, straggling, unorganized line of weary older men and excited young ones. They carried every type of firearm, from machine guns to old flintlock mountain rifles. Some carried banners which said "On to Mingo." Around their necks were tied red bandannas, their union symbol.

The marchers called themselves "red necks." The name, which is now commonly used as a slang term for someone who is uneducated, bigoted, or reactionary, in those days referred to a radical, or "red." It may have had a further meaning to the marching miners, in reference to the red neckerchiefs.

By the afternoon of the 25th, between 7,000 and 9,000 tired marchers overran the

Encampment of federal troops near the Blair Mountain battlefield, September 1921. The soldiers' mission took on the air of a holiday outing, as they encountered no resistance from the miners. Photographer unknown.

twin towns of Madison and Danville in Boone County. The miners cut telephone lines and emptied the stores of food, shoes, and ammunition as they awaited trains to take them to Blair Mountain.

By the early morning hours of Friday, August 26, another group of miners, 1,200 strong, had managed to reach Blair Mountain. There they stole a train which was backed 15 miles up the line to Madison, where the main body of marchers waited for transportation.

As soon as the march had begun, panic broke out in Logan and Charleston. Governor Morgan wired President Harding for federal troops to end the disturbance. Harding responded by sending a military advisor, Gen. H. H. Bandholtz, to assess the situation and end the conflict if possible.

As soon as Bandholtz arrived in Charleston he met with the governor and was briefed on the situation. He then ordered

union leaders Keeney and Mooney to meet with him. The pair was ordered to end the march and disperse all of the participants to their homes at once. Failure to do so would force Harding to send in troops and declare martial law.

Keeney and Mooney arrived in Madison on the afternoon of the 26th, about the same time as the hijacked train. There they found thousands of men lying under trees and propped against buildings, waiting for something to happen. The two leaders herded 600 men into the ball field in West Madison and read the President's order to them. The miners argued and grumbled, but in the end agreed they couldn't fight the entire United States Army and voted to disband.

From the Martin Hotel in Madison, Keeney and Mooney issued the following order to all miners: "This is to certify that the men voted today at 2:30 p.m. in the ball

park to return home. Trains are being arranged for their transportation home."

On Saturday, August 27, the *Gazette* reported the miners homeward bound, and stated: "The March on Mingo County which started as a protest against martial law . . . is now history." Or so they thought.

On the morning of Sunday the 28th word passed like lightning up and down the line of returning men that Sheriff Chafin's guards were shooting women and children in Sharples, a small mining camp just inside Logan County on the Blair Mountain road. Immediately the men turned and started back toward the mountain. Again the sirens were sounded in Logan. The miners regrouped at Blair in less than 36 hours.

What had actually occurred was that Chafin and Captain Brokus, head of the Logan state police detachment, decided to cross Blair Mountain with 200 men and make some ill-timed arrests at the town of

Battle map: The Battle of Blair Mountain was actually fought along an extended front, with Blair Mountain itself being only one point of conflict. In late August and early September angry miners tried to fight their way into the Guyandotte watershed above Logan, contesting major mountain crossing places from Blair Mountain to the northwestward.

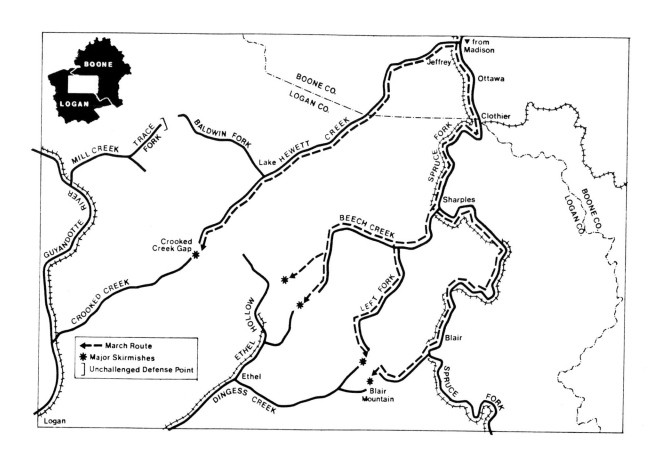

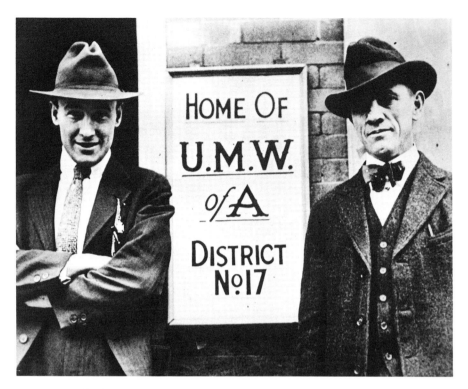

Union leaders Fred Mooney and Frank Keeney balanced precariously between the militant demands of the miners and General Bandholtz's orders to disperse.

Miflin, near Sharples. As the men came down Beech Creek in the darkness they were surprised at Monclo by a group of union men who were still in the area. A pitched battle broke out which lasted for some hours. Two miners were killed and one was wounded. A Logan justice of the peace, Fulton Mitchell, his brother Lucian, and two other deputies were captured by the miners.

Mrs. Maggie Holt, 93, of Sharples, described in an interview how she and her children lay on the floor of their house in Monclo as bullets ripped through the walls and windows. She says she was "scared to death." A neighbor finally came and led them to his house.

The next morning she found a high-powered rifle lying in front of the house. She carried the gun inside and hid it under her "divanette." Miners from Cabin Creek, searching the house for firearms, discovered the rifle and confiscated it.

By the next day Blair Mountain was a raging battle line. Fighting was heaviest at three points where roads crossed the ridge. These places were above Blair town, where the main road crossed, at Beech Creek near Sharples, where a horse trail wound over the mountain, and at the head of Craddock Fork of Hewett Creek, where an old road crossed over onto Crooked Creek near Logan.

Hewett Creek flows into the Little Coal River at the town of Jeffrey in Boone County. It was here that union leaders made their headquarters. Miners coming up from Madison on the commandeered trains would either alight at Jeffrey and walk six or seven miles up Hewett Creek to Blair Mountain, or ride on to Sharples or Blair town before getting off.

With the fight on and thousands of angry miners attempting to cross Blair Mountain, Sheriff Chafin sent out an appeal for help to neighboring counties. Men soon began arriving from the nonunion areas of Mercer, McDowell, Cabell, Wyoming and Mingo counties. Also the state police sent in men. The defenders on Blair Mountain wore white scarves to distinguish themselves from the red neck miners.

Logan was transformed into a military camp and women began cooking in churches and schools to feed the hungry men.

Chafin even resorted to offering prisoners in his ever-crowded county jail freedom if they would go help the defenders on top of the ridge. One prisoner, a bricklayer, was ordered to take a rifle. He refused and, according to another prisoner, was shot and killed. The *Logan Banner* reported that he was shot "while trying to escape."

By Tuesday, August 30, the situation was completely out of hand. President Harding issued a proclamation commanding all "insurgents to disperse and retire peacefully to their respective homes, by 12:00 o'clock noon of the first day of September 1921 and hereafter abandon said combinations and submit themselves to the laws and constituted authorities." Unless they disbanded he would send in federal troops.

The marchers refused to lay down their arms, fearing they would be slaughtered by Chafin's men if they did so. Also, they had amassed their strength at the Craddock Fork of Hewett Creek near Lake, and thought they were about to break over the mountain onto Crooked Creek which leads into the town of Logan. They knew that if they could break through, the defenders would have a difficult time stopping them.

Sheriff Chafin in desperation hired private airplane pilots at $100 a day to fly over the miners and drop homemade bombs on them. The bombs were made out of four- to six-inch oil well casing. Most of the bombs were dropped over Hewett Creek and failed to explode. One which did go off was aimed at a one-room schoolhouse the miners were using as a hospital, on Craddock Fork near Lake. The bomb missed the school by about 100 yards and exploded harmlessly in a field, making a crater large enough to hold a wheelbarrow. No one was reported injured by the bombs.

Milton White, a miner from Boone County who was drafted to fight on the union side, remembers Chafin land mines on the top of the mountain made of cases on dynamite.

The Battle of Blair Mountain by now was making front page news over the world and war correspondents were sent in by major newspapers. One correspondent who had served in World War I wrote that the scene reminded him of Belgium, as refugees fled in panic from the battle area into Boone County.

Boyden Sparks, a famous war correspondent for the *New York Tribune*, was dispatched to the scene with a female reporter who was to report on human interest stories. Chris Holt, who was 15 at the time, remembers that the lady was wearing a pair of riding jodhpurs which "caused almost as much of a sensation in Sharples as the battle." He loaded the reporters into his father's Baby Overland automobile and drove them to the front lines, where he left them. While attempting to reach the Logan lines their group was fired upon and Sparks was wounded in the leg. Holt remembers they were captured and thrown in jail in Logan until they could be identified. He says they wrote some "hair raising" articles about their adventures that weren't complimentary to either jail or jailers.

Special trains carrying food and ammunition were brought in by the UMWA. All local unions were drained of funds to pay for the supplies. Holt remembers his father, who was secretary-treasurer of the Sharples local, writing a check for $1,000 to purchase guns and ammunition.

For a week the battle on the mountain continued sporadically. Lush vegetation of late summer provided a perfect cover for guerilla warfare and individual gun duels,

and much of the action was hidden from view. Doctors and nurses in Boone County were pressed into service by the union to care for the wounded. Dead miners were carried out on the trains, their names and numbers unrecorded. The deaths on both sides have been estimated at between ten and 30, with many more wounded.

It is estimated that at least 10,000 men engaged in the battle. Even though Chafin's men were grossly outnumbered, they had the advantage of strongly fortified positions, several machine guns, unlimited ammunition, and an organized command.

"General" Bill Blizzard, president of Subdistrict 2 of UMW District 17, was generally regarded by the miners as their leader, but the men were too disorganized and strung out to respond effectively to his orders. One miner said, "If the union had only organized and concentrated its forces it could have broken through easily." The miners almost pushed through to Crooked Creek once during the week, but were driven back at the last moment. The citizens of Logan panicked, and the *Banner* published Tennyson's poem, "The Charge of the Light

Brigade," to urge on the defenders.

President Harding's proclamation was dropped to the miners by airplane. When his deadline to cease fighting came and passed unheeded, he called for troops to be sent in from Kentucky, Ohio, and New Jersey. Also, a squadron of army planes was dispatched from Langley Field, Virginia. The planes were armed with gas bombs and machine guns, but were not used. One crashed in Nicholas County and got as much front page coverage in the *Gazette* as did the battle.

When the federal troops arrived in Charleston, they found the streets decorated with flags and lined with cheering crowds. The men were loaded into boxcars and rushed off in the direction of Logan. Another group of soldiers was dispatched toward Logan by way of Huntington and Guyandotte River.

The troops arrived in Madison at night and were met by Bill Blizzard, who introduced himself. He was ordered to call a cease fire and send the miners homeward. He disappeared into the night and by the next morning, September 3, when troops

Angry miners pass near Boone-Logan border on a hijacked train. Photographer unknown, 1921.

A federal encampment on Peach Creek, outside Logan town, on September 6, 1921. POSTCARD VIEW, COURTESY DON CHEEK

arrived at Sharples, the miners were coming out of the hills without guns or red scarves. They were simply a group of dirty, unshaven men trying to get home.

Their guns were hidden all over the mountain; in caves, under leaves, and behind fences. Cush Garrett of Lake, who was a boy at the time, remembers a friend finding a large number of rifles wrapped in a blanket behind a fence. It is reported that rifles are still occasionally found in the area of Blair.

The army set up camps up and down the Little Coal River to preserve the peace, but the fight was over and the union had suffered a crushing defeat.

A grand jury was convened in Logan County and indictments were handed down against Frank Keeney, Fred Mooney, Bill Blizzard, and 982 others, charging them with "murder, conspiracy to commit murder, accessory to murder, and treason against the State of West Virginia."

Immediately the round-up of prisoners began in the surrounding counties. Hundreds were arrested and taken to Logan where every attempt was made to obtain confessions. The trial for treason was moved to the courthouse in Jefferson County, where John Brown had been convicted of treason in 1859. An appeal was sent out across the nation to raise money for the miners' defense fund and over $50,000 was donated.

The major union leaders who had participated in the march were acquitted through lack of evidence and a friendly jury. It was for the lesser figures in the drama to be found guilty and sentenced. One such pair was the mountain preacher and minister J. W. Wilburn and his son John, of Boone County. They had joined the miners' cause only at the last minute, declaring, "It is time to lay down the Bible and take up the rifle." For their minor part they were sentenced to 11 years in the penitentiary. Others were also sentenced to similar prison terms. Governor Morgan paroled them in 1925.

The coal companies had won the battle but would lose the war. After Blair Mountain, the union disappeared in southern West Virginia, not to return until 1933, when New Deal legislation guaranteed the right to organize. But the spectacular Battle of Blair Mountain provoked inquiries into conditions in the coalfields, probing that would go on quietly after the shooting stopped.

Congress investigated, and the outside press took an interest. An article in the *Washington Star* identified Sheriff Don Chafin and his tactics as the main cause of the uprising. Public opinion was shifting, and the marching miners—or their children and grandchildren—would win in the end.

Colorful General Billy Mitchell brought the army planes from Langley Field.
COURTESY WEST VIRGINIA STATE ARCHIVES

The Don Chafin Era

■ By Russell Fogelsong

After growing up in Kanawha and Fayette Counties, Russell Fogelsong spent his early working years in Logan County. There he was an eyewitness to the last episodes of the mine wars, viewing events from the anti-union side. He offers the following first-hand account of the notorious Don Chafin reign in Logan. Don Chafin was the perennial sheriff of Logan County, from about 1910 until after the United Mine Workers of America succeeded in unionizing the Logan District.

Don was a native of Logan County. He was fearless and exercised practically perfect control over every inhabitant of his area. His headquarters were in the town of Logan, his deputies consisting largely of men related to the Chafin clan, either by birth or by marriage. The deputies were spread out, probably one to each of the larger coal camps and one to each group of smaller mines. One squad was maintained in Logan, centering around the courthouse, with each deputy heavily armed and in constant communication with Don's headquarters.

The Logan County Coal Operators Association, of which C. W. Jones of Henlawson was treasurer, was supplemented by a certain amount on each ton of coal mined. I can recall checks going out regularly for the maintenance of the "super-government" headed by Don Chafin. It was Chafin's duty not only to maintain peace and arrest law-breakers, but also to keep a careful ear tuned for any "agitators," meaning union sympathizers, who were promptly fired from their jobs and removed from the Logan District.

The Kanawha District had been unionized after the 1902 strike, and the Cabin Creek area was probably the hot bed of UMW activities. The union, headed by Bill Blizzard for most of the time, was just about as efficient in locating and routing anti-union individuals or groups as was Don Chafin in stopping union activity along the waters of the Guyan River.

The unionized Kanawha River area was separated from Logan County's Guyan River area by high, rugged hills. The Big Sandy drainage, including Mingo and McDowell counties of West Virginia and the border areas of Eastern Kentucky, was even more isolated. The C&O Railroad served the area drained by the Kanawha and Guyan rivers, and the Norfolk & Western served the Big Sandy country. The N&W area was strictly nonunion, as was Logan County.

There were no passable highways across the mountain ranges, and no roads suited to auto traffic even between Charleston and Huntington. Such roads as existed washed out with every heavy rain. Automobiles began to make their appearance early in the century, mostly Ford Model T's with another type here and there. All of this, especially the terrain and roads, serves to indicate why union and non-union areas could be located within a few miles of each other.

One outstanding incident was when the American Civil Liberties Union interested itself in the "desperate plight of the Logan County miners" and dispatched a day coach filled with union sympathizers and trained organizers from New York City. They made it to Huntington and their car was switched onto the Logan passenger train without being detected. But it happened that one of our prominent coal operators, John Kelley, while riding in the chair car on the rear of the train, got wind of the ACLU group.

Mr. Kelley had the train stopped at a small station not far up the Guyan, where it was held until he could communicate with Don Chafin. Don assembled probably 50 of his gunmen, and when all was in readiness the train proceeded to the Logan station. It was allowed to stand there until Don's men could get aboard, spread themselves through the aisles and on the car platforms, and make themselves obvious. It didn't take long for the New York group to realize what was going on and as the train

Sheriff Don Chafin ruled Logan County on behalf of the coal industry. Photographer and date unknown.
COURTESY WEST VIRGINIA COLLECTION, WVU

proceeded beyond Logan, windows were raised and all the firearms in the possession of the ACLU were thrown out the windows. Not a man made any attempt to get off the train, which made its turn around as usual and headed back to Huntington. I assume their car was attached to a train going east, minus the Chafin men who had shepherded them so faithfully along their sojourn into Logan County.

In this connection, I am glad to say that so long as people kept their union ideas to themselves they led a very peaceful life. Of course, a feudal system existed where the companies reserved the right to hire and fire at will, but wages were comparable to the unionized areas, and schools and overall living conditions were good at most mines.

The Logan and N&W areas were, of course, continual irritants to union headquarters in Charleston. In the early 1920's Mother Jones, who was a fiery speaker and agitator, appeared on the scene. She was welcomed by the union and immediately set

Sheriff Chafin, front and center, with deputies at the Logan Courthouse. The huge force was subsidized by the Logan County Coal Operators Association. Photographer and date unknown. COURTESY STATE ARCHIVES

to work to inflame the minds and hearts of all union men. Meetings were held throughout the Kanawha District, but centering on Cabin Creek. The flames were fanned to the point that a ragtag army undertook to unionize the Logan District by force of arms. The miners all wore red handkerchiefs around their necks, thus giving rise to the term "red neck" being applied to any union sympathizer.

When Don Chafin got word of the approaching invaders, he not only assembled his deputies, but also every company man, foreman, and office worker. All took their positions on Blair Mountain. The larger coal companies, including our own, maintained a well-stocked arsenal of rifles and ammunition, presided over by an ex-West Virginia state trooper in the company's employ. I was visiting relatives in Greenbrier County when I got the message that all hands were needed on the job, notwithstanding that I was a cripple and not a fighting man.

Accounts of the fighting were greatly exaggerated, but I believe that one or two men on our side were slightly wounded. There was a considerable amount of shooting, but I don't think either side had the stomach for out-and-out battle. Anyway, Governor Morgan asked for federal troops to be sent in on the Logan side, whereupon the army of red necks beat a rather hasty retreat. That according to my recollection was the sum total of The Battle of Blair Mountain.

Early in the 1930's, Franklin D. Roosevelt was elected president, and he immediately made a deal with union president John L. Lewis. The backing of the federal government took all the wind out of the sails of those opposing the union, and District 17 of the UMW was handed to Lewis on a platter. This was the end of the Don Chafin era.

BLAIR MOUNTAIN NAMED SIGNIFICANT HISTORICAL SITE

The site of the Battle of Blair Mountain, located on W. Va. Route 17 between Blair and Ethel in Logan County, was entered upon the National Register of Historic Places in early 1981.

The four-acre site on top of Blair Mountain commemorates the fierce warfare that raged along nearby slopes, ridges and crests from August 31 to September 4, 1921, between union miners and local vigilantes armed by coal operators. This fighting continued until federal forces, brought in at the request of Governor Ephraim F. Morgan, arrived and the miners were forced to withdraw. The Battle was the culminating event of the post-World War I struggles by members of the United Mine Workers to gain union recognition and better working conditions in the coalfields of West Virginia.

The National Register of Historic Places is kept by the National Park Service. Entry on the Register certifies that the Battle of Blair Mountain was a significant event in American history, and provides the site a degree of protection from federally funded or federally licensed projects. Nomination to the Register was prepared by the Historic Preservation Unit of the West Virginia Department of Culture and History and approved by the Archives and History Commission.

The Siege of Crooked Creek Gap

■ INTERVIEWS BY MICHAEL M. MEADOR ■ PHOTOGRAPHS BY RICK LEE

The events of late summer 1921 are vividly recalled by people living along the main line of march and in the Logan County battle zones. Many fled the area, while others watched in fascination as milelong processions of miners arrived on foot, by automobile, and by hijacked trains. Remembering residents appear to have been sympathetic to the marchers, and many took up arms in their cause.

Early Ball and Cush Garrett live in Lake, at the forks of Hewett Creek in Logan County. Both lived in the community in 1921, with Ball teaching school nearby and Garrett himself a schoolboy. In late August they watched the union invaders tramp up Hewett, then turn left up Craddock Fork to attempt a crossing into nonunion territory at Crooked Creek Gap. From the Gap, it was only a short march down to the Guyandotte River near Logan town, and many observers felt the angry miners had their best chance to break through at this point. In these conversations with Michael Meador, Ball and Garrett recount why the unionists failed to make the planned dawn crossing, and Ball remembers the hectic night before, when he served as the miners' "generalissimo."

Michael Meador. How many days were the men up here fighting?

Early Ball. I couldn't tell you that. They kept moving in closer. The first time I heard of them they were over at Marmet and then kept moving this way.

I was a single man then and lived up the hollow here, pretty well where they were fighting. I was at home with my dad. Everybody was leaving the head of this creek, going down toward Boone County where they had relatives and family to keep them. I drove hundreds of people out of this hollow in my car.

MM Did you have men in the house with you? Did the miners take over your house?

EB No, they didn't take over the house. They never bothered anything. We owned a farm up there just off the main road a little bit, up the creek here on above Cush Garrett's, on up the left-hand fork, where they

came and took over the schoolhouse, Craddock Fork. They came up there and took it over for barracks.

MM Cush Garrett and I drove up there and looked where the school was and he showed me where the bomb had been

dropped on the school.

EB That was the only one that ever exploded. I saw it drop and saw the dirt fly up.

MM Were the planes very high?

EB I don't know. There was one that went over us, and it was shooting some kind of

"It wasn't just miners," Early Ball remembers. "Men from every walk of life took to the hills with high-powered guns."

Young Bill Blizzard, a radical leader of the United Mine Workers, is usually recognized as the miners' commander at Blair Mountian.

gun, a rifle or pistol or something, and it wasn't very high. We both tore loose with high-powered guns. If we ever hit it, it never made a bobble.

Of course, I aimed to be neutral in the case. To tell the truth, my sympathy was with the miners; still I was not a miner, I was a schoolteacher. Elmer Nelson, a boy from up the creek here, we inspected these lines. We started over to inspect the thugs' line, over in the head of Mill Creek. It had rained and we had moved out on a point where we could look them over. We had field glasses and looked them over and didn't go on down, but if we had went on down we would have been on the other side. They would have captured us. We were in the head of Hewett, on Hewett Mountain, looking down Mill Creek. Mill Creek is on the other side going on the right-hand fork.

MM Were they up on top of the divide there?

EB *They were everywhere.* There weren't any miners in that section, but they didn't know when they would come. The miners were all up the left-hand fork, about 5,000. That never was published in the papers. They never mentioned Hewett Creek or nothing like that.

They just come and come all day. It wasn't just miners, there were men come up there from every walk of life—doctors, lawyers, people that run drugstores and got out of there and took to the hills with high-powered guns with the expression, "I want to get a crack at those S.O.B.'s."

MM Do you know anybody that got killed or how many were killed?

EB I don't know. I saw them bring one in but he did not get killed, he had a heart attack. He was carrying water to them. I saw a Negro shot through, but if he died they never brought him into the barracks there.

MM Do you know who was in charge of the miners?

EB Yes, Bill Blizzard.

MM Was he stationed at the schoolhouse?

EB No, he was just in and out. Bill Blizzard was supposed to be the commander-in-chief of them. Whether he was or not I don't know. He came in there a lot.

MM Do you know anything about what happened over at Beech Fork, Ardrosson, or any of those places?

EB Just hearsay is all I know. These fellows they called "thugs," they were hired men and a lot of deputy sheriffs and everything. Don Chafin was a very popular man. We differed politically and everything. Personally I liked him and he was a fine man in my book. He just got rich. He was a good-looking man, a very brainy man, a man who wouldn't lie to you. I heard of him accused a lot, but never knew of him doing anything wrong. I was a "dyed-in-the-wool" Republican here in Logan County and my father, brothers, and both grandfathers. We were a Republican family. There never was one of us mistreated by him. But there were various stories about it, and I can't say whether it was true or not. I don't know.

Now I had a sister who was married and it was reported to me that she was in the basement of the house and had nothing to eat but canned stuff. I decided to go get her.

I went down the road here, I got an army, I had Elmer Nelson with me. When we got up on Craddock Fork the machine gun started cutting the papaw bushes down. We took the other side of the point and went into the hills. We met a crew who had a Thompson machine gun. We pulled in Crooked Creek Gap. There was a Browning machine gun, we were going to capture it. We found out they had moved the machine gun and the bullets were coming through the trees there just a little over our heads. It was a continual fire.

MM Were you up the Sycamore Fork side?

EB I was on the Sycamore, right in the very head of the hollow, almost on the top of Crooked Creek Mountain. I think we had nine men when we got there, out of about 40 or 50. The others took cold feet, you know, dropped out. I had got the news that my sister had come out of there about daylight that morning. So when she got out, I said I don't have anything in this, I'm going home. Some of the boys went on to the other mountain, sight-seeing and so forth.

MM So you stayed up there the whole time then?

EB No, I was all over the world. I went through the line and far down as we could find men and everything.

MM What did they do for food?

EB They had plenty of food, they brought it in here. They never took anything from anybody that I know of. I think they got some stuff on credit at a few stores, but I think they paid for it later. I don't think they beat anybody, but I'm not sure. I was not in business at that time. There were men from every walk of life in this, but they were all called miners.

MM Did you go to Charles Town to the trials?*

EB I was indicted in 700 cases, I guess—not that many but several. We were to give bond that day. I don't know how much bond there was, but I think I give a $200,000 bond then, if they requested it. When they called my name, Don Chafin called across the room to me and said, "Early, don't move your trial, I'll take care

*The Miners' March trials, beginning in late April, 1922, were held outside the coalfields, at Charles Town in Jefferson County. A special train, dubbed the "Red Special" brought union leaders and defense attorneys, as well as 1,000 witnesses and defendants, from Charleston. —ed.

*Mr. Ball recalls his preparations to lead a dawn attack on Crooked Creek Gap.
"I was an ex-Army man, I knew how to fight. I put guards out all over the country."*

of you." Well, that was the law and the gospel, whatever Don told you was the truth. He didn't lie to you.

MM You were indicted or just going to be a witness?

EB I was indicted. I was the "general-issimo" of that army one night. They told them that I knew every crook and turn in that mountain. The miners were told that, and it was put to me [to lead them] or else. Of course, I was going to save Early. I was in it against my will. I was an ex-Army man. I knew how to fight them. I put guards out all over the country, stayed up all night and going around like "Old Cornstalk" telling my men to be brave.

I had 1,000 men lined up to take the Gap the next day at daylight. We had a six-inch cannon that shot explosive balls, and [machine gunner] "Davy Crockett" had moved in a knob there and cleared it, had run everything off. Judge Chambers told me he had fought in the Argonne Forest, but, said that was a living hell on earth when "Davy Crockett" opened up with his machine gun. When the soldiers came in here they wanted to know who was running the machine gun. They were told "Davy Crockett"; but that's what they call him. I never did know his name.

MM You were set up to lead them over the mountain?

EB I was the commander-in-chief for one night, and the next day before we got ready to go Big Lewis White came in. He lived around here at Ottawa and was a high-powered man in the union. He told them that soldiers were coming in up both the Guyan Valley and Coal River, and they would take over and do the right thing. He told them to go into the mountains and tell the men to come in. Big Lewis White came there and told them to come out of the mountains, and not buck the soldiers, that they would do the right thing about it. I never heard anything that done me as much good as that did in my life.

MM Do you think you could have broken through the top of the Crooked Creek Gap?

EB A thousand men could have went through either side of it. You could take soldiers that have to go, they go in. I say this, if they ever got into Logan they would have went through the Crooked Creek Gap, but still it never got a write-up in the papers or anything.

There were people there getting the news, from the *Gazette* and *Daily Mail*. They would get it off [Petrel] O'Dell and myself and go back and print something else. We got this man off to himself and told him, "You fellows come over here inspecting this and are going back writing it up in the paper not what it is. You're going to write it up like it is or we're going to beat you to death when you come back here." I said "You just take your choice. If you write up a lie like you've been doing, we'll whip you." It came out in the paper the next day just like it was.

MM What were they going to do once they got across the mountain?

EB They were going on into Mingo County and turn some prisoners loose they had over there.

MM They were going to take the union on into Logan and Mingo?

EB Yes, they were going to be joined by other union men when they crossed the mountain. That's where they were headed for, but they had to go through Logan. Chafin had decided to stop them on Blair Mountain.

MM If they made it over the mountain here do you think they could have been able to make it through Logan County?

EB I don't know whether they would or not. Don Chafin was a powerful strong man, and he had the operator's money. I

"I stayed up all night, going around like 'Old Cornstalk' telling my men to be brave,"
Mr. Ball continues. "I had 1,000 men lined up to take the Gap at daylight."

know that. When I went up to Charles Town as a witness, they had summoned me, and I told them all I knew would be in favor of the miners. I said I would tell the truth. I said that's evidence in favor of them, and that's what I would have to tell on the witness stand. Well, they took me up there and kept me three or four weeks and some fellow had the miners' money, and don't you think we didn't spend it. He dished it out to us as we wanted it, and we spent it while we were in Charles Town.

MM Were you found guilty of anything?
EB No. I was never tried for anything.
MM Did Chafin fix it up for you, do you think?

EB I hadn't done anything.
MM How long were you in Charles Town?
EB I was there three or four weeks. I was there until they took me on the witness stand and Osenton began questioning me. Osenton, the big lawyer.* "Con Chafin—he was the prosecuting attorney—came through and said "You might as well leave Early Ball alone." He says "I know him, and in fact our families have married into each other." Said, "Early stayed all night with me,

*During the Charles Town trials, Logan lawyers C. W. Osenton and A. M. Belcher were made special assistant prosecutors by Logan County prosecuting attorney J. E. "Con" Chafin. "Con" Chafin and Sheriff Don Chafin were cousins.

slept in my bed, and everything. Whatever Early tells you, truth or lie, he's sharp enough never to change his tale." Said "You just as well quit questioning him, your wasting your time." The next day I was on the train coming home.

Cush Garrett. Like I told you, I was just a boy then and can't remember everything clearly, but I know this much about it. What I heard was that Don Chafin was getting 10 cents on every ton of coal that went out of here, which was hundreds and hundreds of tons. That was to keep the union out.

The union men came to Jeffrey down here on the train from Paint Creek and Cabin Creek. That's where they said they were from. Up the Craddock Fork a short distance there used to be a school, that's where I went to school when I was a boy. I lived up Sycamore, that's a left-hand hollow right above where the school stood. They took that school for their headquarters, the union men did, that's where they did their cooking. Of course, there were so many of them they couldn't sleep in that building, and they asked us to move out of our home up there, which we did. We came to right up there, across the creek. There's a white house up there: that's where my sister lives. At that time it was one of the nicest houses and that's where we stayed while the war was going on.

But the way I understand it the deputies and their outfits was getting the best of the miners. Some of the miners knew a man that was a machine gunner in World War I, and they went and got him and brought him and a machine gun in there. They mounted it on a point where they could zero in on the Crooked Creek Gap, that's where you cross the hill. They said he mowed the leaves off the ground with that thing.

The word came that in two or three days they were going to take Logan, get Don Chafin, and kill him. That's what was told to us here. We had no way of knowing whether it was true or not, but anyway it got bad enough. Don was sheriff at that time, and evidently he called for help because the soldiers came in on the train like the other fellows. They brought some horses with them. They unloaded them and rode them up this creek.

They tried to bomb the headquarters I was telling you about where they took over the school. It must have been some kind of homemade bomb. Used to be I could have taken you up there and showed you the hole. It was about big enough to put a wheelbarrow in and a couple of feet deep.

There was an airplane come over there with two men in it. There were rifles cracking on every side at that thing. You could see the men in there dodging back and forth. It barely cleared this ridge. It was just trying to get away from here, I guess. It wasn't going toward Logan at all. I never will forget that. My cousin and I are about the same age, and we lived pretty close. I stayed with his dad, my mother's brother. We were walking up the road and this airplane, barely over the top of the hill, came over. You could see the men as plain as day. They were scared, you could tell. You couldn't hear for "high powers" cracking.

Men came in here from Paint Creek and Cabin Creek, at least that's where they claimed they were from. They had any kind of gun, just whatever kind of gun they had they brought it. All the soldiers could do if they caught anyone with a gun or weapon was arrest you. Men stuck guns everywhere, just in hollow logs, under rocks or anywhere. I'll bet people around here got 500 or more guns, where some of them would get together and put all their guns together. I can remember my brother-in-law saw the edge of an army blanket sticking under the fence. He pulled it out, and there was a whole bunch of guns. There was one man who left his gun with us, he had a 45-70. It was a big gun but not long-range compared to the modern guns that you have now. He left it, we took care of it, and he came back and got it. He was from over in that section somewhere.

MM Do you have any idea how many miners there were actually fighting?

CG No. They marched up this road. There would be about five or six abreast walking along a little dirt road up here for a mile up and down this road. They were coming in on a train, like I told you, to Jeffrey. They footed it up through here. I don't know how many got mixed up in the actual fighting, but there were lots of men marched from Jeffrey up here besides the ones that maybe came from somewhere else that I didn't know anything about. All I saw were the ones that came up here. Most of the people we saw carrying guns were strangers. We didn't know who they were.

Cush Garrett also has vivid memories of the march. "The word came that in two or three days they were going to take Logan, get Don Chafin, and kill him," he recalls. "That's what was told to us here."

All you knew was what they told you. There were some local boys here, and they actually put my uncle in jail.

MM Because he wouldn't testify?

CG That's right. My daddy left here to keep from getting involved in it. We moved away and stayed for two or three years. We moved into Ohio and stayed in two different places. That was a long time ago. Then we moved across on the West Virginia side down about 16th Street, West, in Huntington. We weren't in the town of Huntington, we were out back of it. My uncle owned a house there, and we moved in and stayed a while until things cooled down.

United Mine Workers President John L. Lewis had his hands full with militants within the union. Here he poses between Blizzard and Keeney at the Jefferson County Courthouse during trials arising from Blair Mountain.
COURTESY WEST VIRGINIA STATE ARCHIVES

Gunmen Resort to Use of Bombs to Kill Women and Children of West Virginia

Bomb Used by Gunmen Against West Virginia Miners

The above photograph was sent to the Journal from West Virginia with the following letter:

"I am sending you a picture of a bomb that was used by the thugs and gunmen of Logan county against the miners in their recent struggle. The bomb was dropped at Jeffery, W. Va., a village in Boone county, not on the camps of the miners, but back in the mining town and country villages, among the women and children. This bomb consists of a gas pipe about two feet long and five inches in diameter, containing about seven pounds of black gunpowder and high explosives. This bomb was manufactured, using a small piece of gas pipe, screwed in one end of the bomb, about six inches long and one inch in diameter, through which a plunger was supposed to work, so that when the bomb hit anything it would drive this plunger back on the detonator, which would explode the bomb. It was also equipped on the rear with wings to guide it through the air, so that it would be sure to strike with the plunger downward.

"This bomb was dropped by gunmen from an airplane on September 1, 1921, but failed to carry out the hellish work intended, which was to blow up innocent women and children of Jeffery. Some twenty or twenty-five others were dropped, many of which exploded, but did no material damage, as the aim of the party dropping them was not accurate and they failed to strike the spot intended."

Stopping the Armed March

The Nonunion Resistance

■ BY JOE W. SAVAGE

The epic struggle for control of the coalfields is usually told from the miner's viewpoint. The following account by the late Joe Savage takes the opposite perspective. Mr. Savage, who fought on the side of the nonunion forces, was a reporter and freelance writer who originally prepared this piece for The New Yorker. *They declined to use it, and the manuscript lay unpublished until son Lon Savage brought it to* GOLDENSEAL *decades later.*

The article was published under Joe Savage's original title in the fall 1987 issue, accompanied by a shorter account by R. B. Adams, also of the antiunion forces.

I first heard of the threatened Mine War in West Virginia one sultry summer afternoon in late August 1921, when I dropped into Mr. Sive's pool room in Charleston to get out of the sun. During that eventful summer I was engaged as a bill collector for a lumber mill, biding my time until the state university re-opened in mid-September. This was a crass kind of job which I would normally have spurned, but my father was a partner in the lumber mill and I could not worm out of the assignment without incurring his displeasure. As it turned out, the job was not so bad. I pedaled up and down the business streets on the tall, black company bicycle, wheedled a few dollars here and there from delinquent debtors, and learned to shoot a fairly creditable game of pool at Mr. Sive's establishment. In time I became interested in a friendly young lady, and had saved enough money to purchase a secondhand canoe when the Mine War disrupted my tenuous schemes of lovemaking on the moonlit Kanawha River.

On this particular afternoon the pool hall was almost empty. I sat alone, comfortably ensconced in one of the high, bulky armchairs and puffed away on a Wheeling stogie. Presently Mr. Sive came around from behind the counter and poured water into a smoking cuspidor.

"What has happened to all your pool sharks?" I asked.

"People don't play pool when they got excitement," he replied.

"Excitement?" I queried. "Has someone shot Judge McClintic?" This was a standard gag. Judge McClintic was our federal judge. He made short shrift of Prohibition violators, and there were always rumors of plots to do him in.

"The excitement is at Marmet," Mr. Sive said coldly. "Coal miners are getting ready to take Charleston."

When I attempted to pass off his statement as ridiculous, he advised me that several hundred disgruntled coal miners had set up an armed encampment near Marmet, 12 miles east of Charleston, and were preparing to march on the city. He was very upset and I assuaged his fears to some extent by pointing out that these things were always exaggerated by calamity howlers. When I arrived home for supper, however, I found the afternoon newspaper creased and wrinkled in the porch swing, and smoothed it out to see if there might be a story about this Marmet fiasco. I was somewhat set back to find the front page devoted almost entirely to the miners' assembly; an estimated one thousand Southern West Virginia coal miners had

already gathered at Marmet, and more were said to be on the way.

After perusing the various news items about the Marmet gathering I was disturbed that people were taking it so calmly; this was a serious thing. The miners' assembly was well financed, and equipped with modern firearms and machine guns. A physician and several nurses were said to be in attendance. The miners even had worked out a uniform, consisting of blue jeans, blue shirt and red bandanna neckerchief. Also they were preparing to march on Logan County; not on Charleston, as Mr. Sive had believed. Heavy reinforcements were expected from the Ohio and Illinois coalfields. The leaders of the armed assembly had shown considerable ingenuity by locating the camp where it could readily be seen by partisans arriving on freight and coal trains. In fact a Chesapeake & Ohio water tank was nearby, where the big Malley freight engines filled up before hauling coal trains across the Allegheny divide, and this was expected to facilitate the detrainment of new arrivals. There was a report that the encampment was rapidly filling up with out-of-state recruits.

When my father arrived home I informed him of this treasonable assembly within veritable cannon shot of the state capitol. To my surprise he was unusually well informed on the subject. He told me the purpose of the assembly was to build up an armed force and march across the mountains into Logan County. Once there, the armed marchers intended to establish the authority of the United Mine Workers of America to negotiate wage contracts between miners and mine owners. I learned later than union organizers who had ventured into the Logan Field for that purpose usually returned with blacked eyes and bruised bodies.

The next morning coal miners began to pour in from nearby states, and on August 24 an estimated 7,000 well-armed miners marched on Logan County. The Armed March, as it came to be known, was officially under way. Led by competent officers, the miners' army moved southward along Lens Creek, crossed over Lens Creek Mountain, came down on Coal River, and bivouacked around the baseball grounds at Racine. Numerous coal company stores were reportedly broken into and robbed during the night, and large quantities of food, arms and ammunition were taken. The next morning Brigadier General H. H. Bandholtz, former Provost Marshall of the American Expeditionary Forces in France, arrived in Charleston to survey the situation for President Harding.

With the arrival of General Bandholtz the Armed March began to falter and many of the miners started back to their homes. However the vanguard pushed on, met up with a force of Logan County deputies on Peach Creek, and five miners were reported killed in the skirmish that followed. Within a few hours the stragglers were back on the Logan trail and a clash occurred near Sharples on Coal River in which seven men were said to have been shot down. Governor Ephraim Morgan of West Virginia wired President Harding and asked that federal troops be sent to West Virginia to put down the armed rebellion. President Harding called on the miners to lay down their arms and go home. "We ought not to have a conflict like that which is going on in West Virginia," he told the War College in Washington. "It is due to lack of understanding." Many West Virginians felt the President was putting the case mildly.

By this time I was quite interested in the Mine War, but became handicapped in my efforts to keep up with it. My father's part-ner in the lumber mill had not been entirely satisfied with the results of my collecting efforts, and had suggested that I give him a daily accounting of debtors upon whom I had called, and a report on what they had to say. This lasted for several days and kept me unusually busy, but after supper on Thursday evening, September 1st, my father let me use the family car and I drove down to Mr. Sive's to get the firsthand information.

When I arrived most of the big arm chairs were already occupied, and all the talk was about the Mine War. There was some information that had not appeared in the newspapers. I learned that questionable women had infiltrated the miners' camp, and disease was rampant. Someone said that a fleet of bombers was en route from Wilbur Wright Airfield in Ohio, to drop incendiary bombs on the miners' march. There were reports of atrocities along Coal River, near the Logan County line. Presently Grant Hall hurried in and said that Governor Morgan was calling for volunteers. Someone asked why volunteers were needed.

"To help Don Chafin," Grant said. "He needs a couple of hundred more deputies on Blair Mountain alone.

Don Chafin was sheriff of Logan County. It was said that he received a rake-off from the mine owners for keeping the union out.

"When does Governor Morgan want these volunteers?" someone asked.

"Right now," Grant said. "He was in front of the YMCA talking to some fellows."

This was startling news. I joined several of my compatriots and we walked over to the YMCA to see what was going on. A rather large crowd of young men had gathered in the second-floor lobby and Governor Morgan was moving about, talking to them. Several lesser state officials were also on hand. Jimmy Kincaid was in charge. Jimmy Kincaid was a World War veteran, and had flown Spads in Italy and France. He sat at a small table, conversed with various young men, and seemed to be writing down their names in a Sit Lux notebook. Presently one of the state officials began tapping on the table with a silver dollar. The crowd quieted down and he introduced the Governor.

Governor Morgan was a well-liked and kindly man. He carefully reviewed the miners' infractions of state law and said it was incumbent upon him to act. He said he knew he could depend on the fine young manhood of West Virginia to support his view; with force if necessary. He announced that a special train had been chartered to carry a voluntary group of defenders to Logan, where they would man the ramparts of freedom. The Governor closed by asking all the red-blooded young men present to assemble at the Chesapeake & Ohio railway station at 11 o'clock; "Ready to go," he said grimly.

When Governor Morgan finished his talk, we were advised that he would like to meet each of us personally. A line formed and I joined in for the handshake. After some minutes I reached the Governor and he placed a fatherly hand on my shoulder.

"What's your name?" he asked with paternal warmth.

"Savage," I said. "Buck Savage."

The Governor looked down at Kincaid, who was writing rapidly in the notebook.

"Got it," Kincaid said snappily, and Governor Morgan shook my hand warmly. "Glad to have you with us," he said, and I was moved on.

Grant Hall and I left the YMCA about 10 o'clock. He had also shaken Governor Morgan's hand, and he knew where we could borrow a couple of pistols from a fellow who had been on the police force. The fellow was still up, and loaned each of us a revolver; mine was a .38 caliber Smith and Wesson. We agreed to meet at the station and I hurried home to change into rough clothes. My parents were both sound sleepers, and I managed to don some hunting garb and get out without waking them.

Grant Hall was already on hand when I arrived at the station and we milled about in the crowd. A few stout-hearted state officials passed among us with words of courage. The night train for Washington roared in, running behind schedule, and discharged and took on passengers while harried porters cleared passageways through the throng. Presently the conductor called "all aboard," and the train moved off in a blast of steam.

Almost immediately a train of three passenger coaches, pushed along by a yard engine, backed into the station. "This is it," someone yelled, and we clambered aboard. Presently the engine bell rang, the whistle sounded and our phantom train moved off into the night.

For the first several miles there was much moving about from coach to coach; most of the defenders were curious to learn who the other defenders were. Our coach was in charge of Bud Connell, another war veteran. Two or three men in our coach had thoughtfully brought playing cards along, and a stud poker game was about to get in progress when word came that the lights would be doused at Saint Albans. Saint Albans was the transfer point for the Coal River division of the Chesapeake & Ohio, and it was considered possible that snipers from the miners' army might be lying in wait. The lights went off as we approached the town limits, and Bud Connell posted an armed guard at each end of our coach. The train roared through Saint Albans without incident and clicked along the rails at a steady pace until we neared Huntington. Then we were switched over on the Logan division of the C&O, and headed southward along the Guyandotte River toward Logan. When my turn came as sentry I sat on the coach steps, fingered the Smith and Wesson revolver, and watched the dark countryside roll past. Bud Connell came out to inspect the guard and we had a long talk together. I asked him about our movements when we reached Logan.

"Hell, I don't know any more about it than you do," he said painfully, and ducked back in the coach.

A number of deputies were at the station to meet us when we rolled into Logan sometime after midnight. After much milling around outside the station we were formed into units and marched away. My unit was marched to a lodge hall, and we were told to remain there until further notice. We filed into a large, dimly lit assembly room and found the floor covered with mattresses; with hardly room to move between them. The deputy in charge told us to get as much sleep as possible, and be ready to move out on five minutes notice. He then departed.

For several minutes our unit moved about, most of us trying to avoid an undesirable mattress mate. There were several pulpit-like rostrums around the walls, and an extroverted defender mounted one and delivered a mock lecture. This took the strangeness out of our surroundings, we began to relax, and presently I dozed off alongside a snoring giant from North

The U.S. Army arrives in Logan County. The town of Logan was the jumping off point for wagon and foot travel into the mountains. POSTCARD VIEW, COURTESY DON CHEEK

Charleston.

Our sleep was of short duration. About two o'clock we were aroused and told to fall out in front of the building. In a few minutes we found ourselves marching in double column along the quiet, dimly lighted streets of Logan. Presently we arrived at the courthouse and filed in for the issuance of arms. The courthouse was a veritable arsenal, the wide hallways stacked with Enfield rifles and boxes of ammunition. Each of us was issued a rifle, ammunition, and cartridge belt, and when we emerged in the bluish light of a street lamp a dozen or so Ford taxicabs awaited us. I climbed into one with Ben Reber and some West Side boys, and the car rattled off. We plied the driver with questions about our destination, but he was a taciturn character who probably wished he was elsewhere, and we left him to his thoughts.

The car bumped along a dirt road for perhaps a dozen miles, headlights dimmed and the air chocked with dust. Occasionally we could see the flickering lights of the cars ahead, but there was no sounding of horns; no sound at all except the rattle and thump and wheeze of the car as it threaded its way toward the mountains. At last we saw a flash of light waving ahead and came to a halt. A man with a husky voice told

us to fall out and move forward. We piled out into the darkness, dragging rifles and other gear. As we shuffled forward in the tense blackness, another taxicab came to a halt behind us. The engine backfired, there was a moment of eerie quiet, and someone ahead called "Take it easy—take it easy."

When we reached the front car there were several flashlights moving about briskly like souped-up fireflies. I heard Bud Connell's voice and moved toward it. He was talking softly with two older men; one wore a silvery officer's badge that glittered when swept by beams of light. The man with the husky voice came forward, prodding stragglers from the last two or three cars. Presently we were assembled loosely around the leaders, and the husky-voiced man kept prodding us in closer, like herding sheep toward a loading chute. The man with the deputy's badge began talking. His words were low, but clear and distinct in the cold morning darkness.

"Connell will take you up this ravine," he said, nodding backward with his head. "We've got a patrol up ahead that will direct you up the mountain." He looked out over our group and told us to come in closer. We shuffled around into a more compact group; those of us in front hunched down so the others could tell what was going on.

Volunteer defenders such as these filled the streets of Logan throughout late August and early September. It was the business of the Army to separate them from the union miners on the other side of Blair Mountain. POSTCARD VIEW, COURTESY DON CHEEK

"The password," said the deputy sheriff, "is Holden. Don't forget it."

"Holden," someone repeated.

"Don't say it," the deputy said harshly. "Just remember it."

Presently we moved on, some 30 of us following Bud Connell through the darkness. In a few minutes we stopped while the vanguard felt out the path. In the stillness we could hear the Ford taxicabs rattling along on their return to Logan. We moved on into the cold, quiet night, sometimes inching through shallow water at a snail's pace, often brushed by alder and willow limbs, always listening for whispered sounds ahead. We had just emerged from particularly difficult terrain where thorny shrubs tore at our clothing when a flashlight beamed ahead and a shrill, excited voice called "Halt!"

We stopped at once and waited tensely. No other words were spoken, no command given. The stillness was painful. Across the small creek we heard the metallic click of rifles being cocked ready to fire. The voice called again, "Advance your leader."

Bud Connell moved forward awkwardly with the flashlight shining on his face. We heard muffled voices. Then Bud called softly and we moved up. "Don't be so slow with that password," we heard someone say.

We huddled about and the fellow in charge of the patrol told us we were at the base of Crooked Creek Mountain. "The reason you don't hear any shooting," he said, "they save their ammunition for daytime. You fellows better get up there before it starts."

He and Bud Connell conversed quietly for a few minutes; then we began the long climb to the top. This was more tiring, but less frustrating, than the ravine. The mountain slope was fairly steep, but we were able to follow a well-worn path until we neared the crest. In the half-light of early morning we began to see great trees silhouetted against the sky; giant oaks, pines, chestnut and beech. Tall saplings grew in profusion. There was little underbrush at this elevation, and soon we were able to see the outline of the ridge. We dragged slowly upward. Mitt Tucker broke a shoelace and we all gathered about, glad for the respite, while he fumblingly tied it together in the nebulous pre-dawn greyness.

It was still a long way from sunrise when we reached the mountain crest; Connell in the lead and the rest of us strung out like Sherpa porters approaching Mount Everest. Suddenly the head of the line halted and a tall, weather-beaten man appeared, seemingly from nowhere, and began talking to Connell. Since we heard no rifle bolts clicking into firing position, we moved up and gathered around this gaunt old-timer. He talked quietly for a minute or two. His name was Gaujot, and he was manning a machine gun, partially camouflaged behind a giant oak. Presently other seasoned defenders appeared and seemed quite glad to see us.

Colonel Gaujot, as he was called, told us to make ourselves comfortable on the sheltered side of the ridge. He said we would be stationed at various possible breakthrough areas as soon as it got light enough to make our way. In the meantime he said to get what sleep we could. We all dropped our gear and stretched out on the near-level mountain top, but no one slept.

It seemed an unconscionably long time before sunup, but at last the dancing light of morning appeared far off on the Eastern summits, and we made ready to move off. This was a fairly simple procedure; we simply stood up, stretched our aching limbs, and lined up in a single file behind Bud Connell. Crows were calling nearby, and smaller birds flitted about through the sparse underbrush. Far to the westward we heard the mooing of a cow. In this peaceful setting we moved out near the crest of Crooked Creek Mountain. Presently we came upon a trail and followed it for a hundred yards or so. In some places we could look out across the far valley and see the opposite range. Suddenly we heard firing off to the right, far across on the next ridge. At once this seemed a relief; I felt that we had not made the long trip for nothing. At least there was some action, even though far away. Then I heard whining noises, like angry bees. Dirt began to spatter up almost underfoot. Small twigs snapped off sapling limbs and spiraled downward. The man in front of me staggered and fell, and went crawling downward out of range. Colonel Gaujot's machine gun opened up and we suddenly realized we were under attack. We broke and fled headlong down the mountainside to safety.

As soon as we were out of danger, Bud Connell began rallying our forces and presently most of us were together again. The man who had fallen was shot in the buttocks. We helped him maneuver into a not-too-painful position on his stomach, and later he was taken down the mountain, lying face down across a mule.

In the relative safety now afforded us by the mountain crest, our courage quickly returned. We moved along cautiously below the ridge and presently came upon a group of defenders who were comfortably ensconced in a notch, where the crest dipped downward for a hundred feet or more. There were great rocks about, some as big as trucking vans, and a number of our men were left there to reinforce this somewhat vulnerable defile.

The crest of the mountain began to give way a little farther along, and turned inward toward the miners' forces. Some of us moved cautiously along this salient under scattering fire, and suddenly came upon 10 or 12 young men in a long, narrow fissure in the massive rock formation. This cleft was six to eight feet across, and its depth varied from four to six feet. The defenders who were manning this natural fortification were lolling about smoking cigarettes and telling stories, and plainly looked upon the rest of us as intruders. However, Bud Connell had orders to disperse his men among the defenders, and it fell my lot to join these seasoned 24-hour veterans. I was turned over to a husky, confident fellow named Spurlock, who told me to make myself at home.

From the rim of our protective crevice we could look far down into the valley that separated us from the invaders. A desolate farmhouse could be seen in a small clearing; pole beans and corn were growing in the garden. The farmer's cow had been killed by gunfire and the carcass could be seen through the field glasses, sprawled across the well path. Machine guns sporadically sprayed the area, purportedly to discomfort possible enemy snipers, but more likely to relieve the tension on itching trigger fingers.

Throughout the morning there was intermittent rifle and machine gun fire from the other side of the deep valley. We responded in kind, and if the interval between volleys was overly long, someone would fire a few rounds toward the invaders and set off another round of heavy fire. During these outbursts we could hear the comforting tat-tat-tat-tat of Colonel Gaujot's machine gun far up the ridge.

Midday arrived much sooner than expected. I was pumping some lead downward through the trees when a fellow named Jerry Sizemore grasped my arm and told me to lay off. He pointed down the sheltered side of the mountain and I saw two men bringing a pack mule toward us; one leading and the other threatening the animal from the rear. Firing eased up all along the ridge. The two men stopped some 15 or 20 feet below us, extracted a large packet of sandwiches and a dozen or so bottles of pop, and the smaller of the two slithered up to our crevice and delivered our noonday repast. Spurlock called timeout for all but a cadre of riflemen who manned our parapet. The sandwiches were all made with bologna, but the slabs and the bread slices were thick and we made out very well, washing them down with orange, lemon, sarsaparilla and other palatable soft drinks turned out by the Logan bottling factory.

Time slowed up in the early afternoon. Firing was intermittent. Colonel Gaujot's machine gun took a long nap, and something akin to the doldrums settled down on our group; particularly on the seasoned old-timers. Jerry Sizemore said it was the same the day before; "things slacked off after we ate," he confided. Jerry Sizemore was from Lincoln County, and lived with his parents on a small farm near West Hamlin. He told me about his old man selling their cow for $35.

"He changed it in nickels," Jerry said, "and lost every last one in the slot machine at the Griffithsville pool room."

"Every last nickel?" someone asked.

"It took him two days," Jerry said. "We didn't even know where Pa was."

This story was a good morale builder; everyone seemed to relax and several of us sought out isolated spots in our ravine and tried to sleep. I was fairly successful, but about four o'clock heavy firing began from the miners' ridge and we could hear the whine of bullets ricocheting off the trees. Colonel Gaujot's machine gun got back in business, and we all began firing down the slope through the sumac and sassafras where invaders would be most likely to attempt a breakthrough. There was movement and activity below us, and much excitement all along our ridge. Several of our men called out that they could see miners dodging between trees and underbrush, but if invaders were there, they failed to break out into the open and make a frontal attack. About six o'clock the shooting eased off, but far off to the southeast we could hear heavy firing along the Blair Mountain front.

One pleasing aspect of the Mine War was the cessation of hostilities as darkness approached. Firing slacked off before dusk, and soon stopped entirely. Many of us climbed out of our natural defense post and visited other groups of defenders along the ridge. Others scoured about getting firewood, and when the rest of us returned to our bivouac, small fires were burning all along the ridge. Three or four fires were blazing in our ravine, and men were lying about on the ground; some talking, others trying to sleep. I crept between two lanky defenders and put in a restless night.

We were up and about long before dawn, in time to welcome the sandwich men and a handful of reinforcements. The morning was still, moist with dew. Crows were calling down the slope, and westward we could hear the faint tinkle of faraway cowbells. Even our voices seemed to echo from nearby trees. It was the kind of morning one welcomes in farm country, when nature seems at peace.

We greeted the newcomers in high good humor; big bologna sandwiches were distributed, bottles of pop were tossed along from one person to another. One ambitious toss was too high; the bottle went over the parapet and lodged against a sapling. One of the newcomers climbed hastily over the parapet to retrieve the bottle. Suddenly, just like the morning before, we heard the tat-tat-tat-tat of a machine gun from the opposite ridge and the newcomer fell. Jerry Sizemore ran quickly to his side and brought him back under intense fire. The newcomer was pale and apologetic, but unharmed.

In the meantime our defenders all along Crooked Creek Mountain had opened up and a real battle was in progress. Colonel Gaujot was still on the job; up on the ridge his machine gun was barking in angry spurts. We took turns manning our parapet and kept steady fire for at least two hours. Bullets spattered all around us, but we were fairly safe in our natural redoubt.

As the morning wore on, firing on both sides became desultory, and about 11 o'clock the miners' fire stopped altogether. We kept popping away from time to time, but there was no retaliatory fire. I brought out my Smith and Wesson revolver, and several of us took turns shooting at green chestnut burrs in a nearby tree. Word came down from the high ridge that Colonel Gaujot had sent a scouting party down hill, and we were ordered not to fire until further notice. We laid about in the warm sunshine that trickled through the trees and a young man next to me, a fellow named Harless, complained that people were not trustworthy like they used to be. Someone asked him why, and he said he had recently made a deal to sell his car to a mill hand. When the time came to consummate the deal, he said, the mill hand failed to show up. There was silence after this startling denouement, and

This airplane, part of Sheriff Don Chafin's civilian "air force" crashed into a Logan house on August 27. The nonunion forces used planes in reconnaissance and for unsuccessful bombing runs. POSTCARD VIEW, COURTESY DON CHEEK

Harless was nettled. "I had a notion to call him a fine bird," he added, drawing out the word "fine."

Jerry Sizemore, who had appeared humorless in relating his father's experience with the slot machine, was quite different with Harless.

"My God," he said, drawing back, "you wouldn't really have called that fellow a fine bird?"

"The hell I wouldn't," Harless said with vigor.

"That's going too damn far," Sizemore said earnestly, and everyone broke out in laughter. Harless was uncomfortable. He got up, brushed the seat of his trousers, glanced down the mountainside, and suddenly became transfixed.

"In God's name," he cried out. "Does anybody see what I see?"

Two or three of us jumped up, someone let out a yell, and presently pandemonium began to spread all along the ridge. Down the slope we saw a phalanx of U.S. troops toiling up the mountain, accompanied by big, muscular Army mules drawing light artillery field guns. We all jumped up on the parapet and cheered. Everywhere along the ridge, tired defenders came running out of their defense positions and began throwing their hats and yelling. The long crest of the

mountain rang with tumultuous shouts of welcome. Old Warren G. Harding hadn't forgotten us after all.

The troops toiled upward and were soon with us. It was a battalion of infantry from Fort Knox, Kentucky. Many of the soldiers were young boys, grinning and asking what happened to the war. A grizzled buck sergeant of about 35 years was in charge of the three or four squads that prepared to take over our salient. A corporal barked authoritatively at several men who were handling pack mules; the field guns had already been moved farther up to the right, where the crest was higher. Presently a young first lieutenant appeared, wearing highly polished cordovan leggings and a battered campaign hat. He announced that his men were taking over, and we crowded around while he talked with Spurlock. The lieutenant asked some very pertinent questions and Spurlock filled him in with a brief summary of our experience. Spurlock was not overly modest in relating some of our exploits. The lieutenant said few of his men had ever been under fire, and expressed the hope that they would do as well as the civilian defenders.

"I think the miners have cleared out," Spurlock said.

"We'll go get them," the lieutenant said

smugly, and Spurlock looked around at the rest of us knowingly.

We milled around with the soldiers, not knowing exactly what to do. About two o'clock a bristly major wearing whip-cord breeches appeared with two of Sheriff Chafin's deputies and we were told that we were relieved, and could start moving down the mountain. Some of us were reluctant to leave so abruptly, but we were plainly in the way of the troops so we gathered up our scanty possessions and started downward.

Pathways down from the ridge fed into a main trail, and as we moved along we began to meet many of our old friends with whom we had made the trip from Charleston. Young men from Huntington and Welch and Bluefield were having much the same experience; the air was filled with greetings, reunions and loud talk, much like campus encounters after a summer vacation. I met up with Grant Hall again, and we traded lies all the way down the mountain. At last we reached the road where we had been deposited by the wheezing taxicabs. A hundred or so defenders were standing about, and we were advised that more cars would be along soon. We milled around in the dust and sweat until late afternoon, when at last our turn came. Only a few taxicabs were engaged in the return transportation effort, but a number of Logan boosters had manned their family cars and were helping out. We rode in with a horse doctor, who told us Billy Blizzard was getting ready to attack the federal troops with grenades. We asked him who Billy Blizzard was. He withered us with scorn and said Billy Blizzard commanded the Miners' Army.

It was dark when we were deposited at the Aracoma Hotel in Logan. Arms were stacked all about the entrance and a guard was at the door. He asked us for the password and for a moment neither of us could remember it.

"You're the only two men in Logan who don't know it," said the guard, and permitted us to enter.

The lobby of the Aracoma Hotel was like a military headquarters. An Army colonel and several lesser officers were moving about, talking with deputies and state police officers. They all said the Mine War was definitely over. There was a news bulletin that the miners had begun evacuating the

disturbed area about noon, when they learned that federal troops had arrived in Logan. It was reported that they had hastily buried 50 bodies before moving out. A news dispatch said the bodies of two miners had been left on the porch of an undertaking parlor near Marmet. We also learned that a correspondent for the *New York Tribune*, Boyden Sparks, had been shot in the head en route from Blair Mountain to Logan, but was expected to recover.

There was a Red Cross booth in the Aracoma lobby, and after cleaning up in the washroom we paid it a visit. The lady in charge was very solicitous of our welfare and advised us that efforts were being made for a special train to take the Kanawha County men back to Charleston. She filled us up on sandwiches and hot coffee, and we set out to see the town.

It was Saturday night and the pool rooms were full. Logan was overrun with defenders like ourselves, and also with country folks who had come in to the county seat to buy

groceries and see the movies. About 10 o'clock we ran into some of our Charleston cohorts. They advised us that the C&O special train had been arranged for and would leave shortly after midnight. By this time the glamour of victory had worn very thin and we arrived at the station long before 12 o'clock. Most of the Charleston contingent were already on hand, waiting glumly for the Charleston special. Many of the men were lying about on the station benches, and some were sleeping on the floor. About two o'clock a train pulled into the station and we were put aboard. I fell into an empty seat and closed my eyes as the train rumbled off into the night. I dreamed we were back on Crooked Creek Mountain; the miners were breaking through our lines, piling down into our sheltered crevice. Hand-to-hand combat ensued. I went for a miner's throat. He yelled fiercely and fought back. It was Grant Hall. "Get the hell out of here," he said gruffly. "We're home."

Morgan conferred repeatedly with General H. H. Bandholtz, seeking a full-scale military intervention in southern West Virginia. COURTESY STATE ARCHIVES

Blair Mountain from the Other Side

■ BY R. B. ADAMS

*T*hree days before the U.S. Army was ordered into Coal River and Logan to settle the Mine War, our engineering crew was in No. 10 mine at Holden. An emergency call came from Logan for ex-servicemen to report to the courthouse in Logan. As our crew chief, Vic Willis, was an ex-serviceman, we came out to report to the mine manager, W. O. Percival. Mitchell Bower and I—we had been junior high school classmates at Bedford, Virginia—told Percival that we were both ROTC trainees, Mitchell at Fishburne and I at VPI. He told us to go ahead.

When we reached Logan courthouse we were told to line up with the others who had reported. We were then told to go to one of the designated stores and get any clothes needed for the mountain and report back in one hour. Edward "Whitey" Bloom had me change boots and fitted me with a naugahyde jacket. We reported back to the courthouse and Harry S. Walker, Logan Elementary School principal, was appointed captain and Charles J. Everett, Logan hardware salesman, was appointed lieutenant. We were then told our mission.

It seemed a shortcut foot path across the mountain between Ardrosson (abandoned mine no. 4 on the left fork above Monclo) and Ethel (actually Keyes) had been overlooked. It was not known what was happening there and must be investigated. We were loaded into trucks and taken up Bear Wallow Hollow to Keyes on the Logan side of the mountain. We settled long enough to be issued Springfield rifles and clips of ammunition and to load one clip in the rifles. I was also given a Smith and Wesson revolver and led the advance patrol up the mountain. We would advance about 100 feet and signal the next patrols in turn to follow. We reached the top of the mountain without incident and established headquarters. Two-man picket posts were estab-

lished at about 50-yard intervals along the ridge between Blair on the right and Crooked Creek on the left.

A fellow named John Chapin from New York, whom I have never known before or since, and I were the last post on the Crooked Creek side. We made ourselves a den in the brush and took turns in standing watch. During the evening there was sporadic firing in the valley below, the only noise except the dew falling to sound like footsteps in the leaves. Darkness brought quiet except for an infrequent shot in the valley. At daybreak intense firing began.

We were supposed to have been relieved at 7 A.M. After waiting until after 9 A.M. for relief, we decided to follow the picket posts between us and headquarters to find out the situation. We found all picket posts deserted and reported to Charlie Everett that something was wrong. He replied "Hell, yes. When the heavy shooting began at daybreak they all came into headquarters!"

We spent the next two nights as repetitions of the first, quiet at night and heavy fire during the day. Except for a scarcity of food it was a rather uneventful period, Chapin and I never sighting an "enemy." Each time a man was sent off the mountain to inquire about food he did not come back—and rarely any food. We got enough to sustain us, but sometimes the Alex Rose's Bakery bread boxes contained Beechnut chewing tobacco.

After the third night we were notified the U.S. Army troops were in Logan. Trucks were at the foot of the mountain to take us back to Logan, where we found the troops. It was over. I have never understood why the short path across the mountain was not used to reach Logan, unless Bill Blizzard* did not

*Bill Blizzard, a militant officer of United Mine Workers District 17, was recognized as the "generalissimo" of the armed miners invading Logan County. Blizzard and other leaders were later tried for treason against the state, and acquitted.

know about it. The miners' plan may have been to establish intense fronts at Blair and at Crooked Creek, then slip over the shortcut.

All accounts of the Logan Mine War refer to the troops as U.S. Army. At the time I thought some might have been West Virginia National Guard units or volunteers from Welch under the command of Colonel William E. Eubank. I do know that one of the men was a man named "Waddy" Chewning, who had a movie date with a Logan girl with whom I became acquainted. Some accounts state that a Logan unit of the West Virginia National Guard was engaged in the Logan defense forces. This is untrue. The Logan unit was not organized until after the Mine War, when Company E, 150th Infantry, was organized with Harry S. Walker as captain and Charles J. Everett as lieutenant. I was named 1st sergeant, to do the work. Shortly afterwards, Company M, a machine gun company, was formed with Huntington native Joe Corbely of Micco as captain and New York native Ned Crummy lieutenant. I did not re-enlist after my one-year enlistment expired.

As an addendum, before the road had been built across the mountain between Blair and Hetzel I once was traveling from Logan, via train to Saint Albans and then by the Coal River train to Sharples, to call on the Boone County Coal Corporation and spend the night at their clubhouse. On the train I met E. M. Jeffrey, general store manager of Logan Mining Company, who had been on a visit to a small mine operated by J. J. Ross, formerly of Logan. He told me that instead of spending the night he planned to walk across the shortcut path to Ethel and get a taxi into Logan and suggested I join him. It was music to my ears. After we reached Sharples we started up Beech Creek where he stopped and said he wanted to say hello to his son-in-law, who operated an independent store across the creek from the road. Shortly he returned and said his son-in-law had talked him into staying overnight, but that I would have no trouble in finding the path.

Anxious to get home, I started the walk. I wended my way on to Monclo and past Ardrosson to the foot of the mountain where I found the path, but as I traveled up the mountain the path became more indistinct. Finally I reached the top and started down the mountain, wondering where I would reach bottom. An angel saved me. At the foot of the mountain I spied some pipes coming from the head of a gas well. I knew where I was. Several years before I had been invited to witness the shooting of the well, which had been promoted by a man named Comstock of Charleston and drilled by the Wilson brothers. I walked on to Ethel and called a taxi to Logan. It had taken me four hours to make the trip, instead of the supposed one hour. Strangely, five years after the walk across the mountain I returned to Sharples to work for Boone County Coal Corporation.

Troops at Blair Mountain, probably September 1921. COURTESY EASTERN REGIONAL COAL ARCHIVES

BOOK REVIEW

The evening I met Denise Giardina, she read aloud to a group of four or five other writers the beginning pages of what was to become her novel, *Storming Heaven*. For the next three years, we gathered almost weekly. Each week, she read us the latest installment.

Giardina grew up in the West Virginia coalfields. Incredibly, she never heard the story of The Battle of Blair Mountain in her mandatory West Virginia history class in eighth grade, nor in the college-level class that was a prerequisite for a history degree. She first read about the miners' revolt in a book she bought at Major's Bookstore in Charleston. Subsequently, she learned more about early United Mine Workers organizers and the 1921 labor uprising from the children and grandchildren of some of the thousands of miners who took up arms. *Storming Heaven* tells how it happened, and why.

The first chapter of *Storming Heaven* recounts the coal companies' systematic acquisition, often by force or guile, of land and mineral rights in county after county of southern West Virginia. The last paragraph of the book is a single sentence: "The companies still own the land." The story in between Giardina's

contribution to the struggle. For *Storming Heaven* is a war story, and to this novelist the war is not over.

Giardina's story, which takes place in fictional West Virginia and Kentucky counties clearly modeled on Mingo and Pike, is advanced by four narrators: C. J. Marcurn, Rondal Lloyd, Carrie Bishop, and Rosa Angelelli. Marcum is the mayor of Annadel, the only town in the area not owned by coal baron Lytton Dnvidson; Lloyd, a coal miner and union organizer; bishop, a nurse; and Angelelli, an Italian immigrant who works in the household of the company owner. These characters are also four faces of war.

C. J. Marcum embodies the independence of old-stock Appalachians, their deep attachment to the land, and the dignity of the mountain people. In a sense, his is the voice of the generations that lived and worked in the West Virginia mountains before the land was taken. With his friend, black Doctor Toussaint Booker, C. J. forms the Annadel Free Press, joins the Socialist Party, and champions free speech and human rights for the miners. Through C. J., the reader gains an understanding of what his family and so many others have lost.

Rondal Lloyd is the anger and the zeal of war. It is Rondal who directly experiences the grueling life of a child in the mines, and the ordeal of an encounter with company terrorists. From his bitterness is born the hard, unwavering energy of a union organizer.

Carrie Bishop illuminates the courage, as well as the compassion, that may arise out of conflict. Carrie's training as a nurse allows this character to convincingly illustrate the poor conditions in the coal camps, and then to lead the reader into a much more desperate scene, that of the tent camps where thousands of evicted miners, along with their wives and children—those who managed to survive the assaults of typhoid fever, flu, and pneumonia—waited out the cold winter of 1920–21. Carrie's strength and stability derive at least partly from her preindustrial childhood in Kentucky, in the days before coal mining took her part of the mountains. This narrator's descriptions of growing up surrounded by loving relatives (including the unforgettable aunts,

Jane and Becka) are among the most lyrical in the book.

The very different voices of Carrie and Rondal, who narrate the longer passages in the book, balance one another like a passionate, sometimes discordant musical tone.

Finally, there is Rosa Angelelli. Rosa has been moved from her homeland to a foreign place and a way of life that is not what she and her family expected. The reader is introduced firsthand to the unsafe conditions in the mines by Rondal Lloyd, but Rosa's tragedy bears witness to the implications for the women whose husbands and sons work underground. The short chapters narrated by Rosa are haunting, for hers is the voice of grief so overwhelming that it cracks not only the heart, but the mind.

These narrators speak directly to the reader in natural, true voices and they introduce a cast of others. There is the "No-Heller" Preacher Albion Freeman, who declares that his church is deep under the earth; the family of prosperous Ermel Justice, whose sons grow up with Rondal; Carrie's gentle sister Flora and her husband Ben; and the deeply principled Doc Booker, through whom Giardina explores relations between blacks and whites in the union movement.

These people are described in loving detail. Their laughter, their frailties, their games, their passions, the food they eat—their lives, in short—emerge clearly in the voices of Giardina's four narrators.

Storming Heaven is a forceful, fullhearted account. The story moves with the soaring rhythm of old time music. The people who come alive on these pages will not easily leave a reader's imagination.

The author's first novel, *Good King Harry*, showed her to be as skillful a researcher as she is a writer; and her penchant for accuracy broadens this novel of West Virginia history. The events from the Matewan Massacre to The Battle of Blair Mountain have been absent from textbooks for too long.

—COLLEEN ANDERSON

STORMING HEAVEN *is available as a paperback book, published by Ivy Books/Random House. It may be purchased in bookstores for $5.99 or through the order form on page 109.*

Looking Back on
the Mine Wars
The Memories Remain

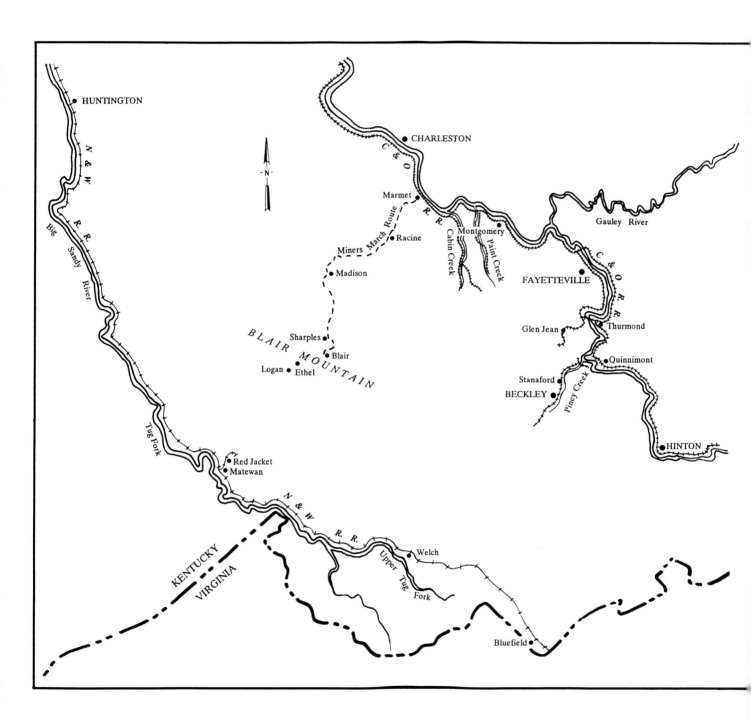

HUNTINGTON

CHARLESTON

C & O

N & W R.R.

Big Sandy River

Marmet

Miners March Route

Racine

Madison

Cabin Creek

Montgomery

Paint Creek

Gauley River

FAYETTEVILLE

C & O R R

BLAIR MOUNTAIN

Sharples

Blair

Glen Jean

Thurmond

Logan • Ethel

Quinnimont

Stanaford

Piney Creek

BECKLEY

Tug Fork

HINTON

Red Jacket
Matewan

N & W R.R.

KENTUCKY

VIRGINIA

Welch

Upper Tug Fork

Bluefield

Mack Jenks, Union Bard

■ By J. Roderick Moore

The marching miners lost the Battle of Blair Mountain, but within a few years they had won the war. With Franklin Roosevelt's election as president of the United States and the subsequent reform of national labor law, organizers swept across the West Virginia coalfields, swiftly bringing all of the state into the union. Today the long struggle lives only in the memories of the aging men and women who participated and in the stories they have handed down.

Some of the best, most durable stories come to us in the form of songs. Two of the most prolific songwriters from the late organizing period were Orville and Mack Jenks of McDowell County. J. Roderick Moore's 1977 interview with Mack explores this period and the relationship of the songwriting brothers.

Although I spent most of my life in Welch, West Virginia, it wasn't until 1971 that I was introduced to the music of West Virginia coal miners. Like many other residents of McDowell County, I was more familiar with polkas, pop songs, and country sound that saturated the radio waves than I was with our traditional music. It was at the Middle Atlantic Conference on Folk Culture in Pittsburgh in 1971 when I first met Dr. Archie Green, author of the book, *Only a Miner*. When he learned I had spent some time working in the mines and had been a UMWA member, he automatically asked if I was familiar with Orville Jenks. I had to admit that while I recorded some black music in West Virginia, I had done no work with mining songs.

Somewhat chagrined, I began to make inquiries about the Jenks family and posted a notice in the Welch newspaper that I was looking for information about Orville Jenks. Almost immediately I heard from Orville's daughter Ruby and his brother Mack who invited us to come out and talk about Orville. In his book on mining music, *Minstrels of the Mine Patch*, George Korson had mentioned Orville but not his brother Mack. It was with some surprise that I learned that Mack was also a singer and songwriter. On December 30, 1971, in a two-hour interview, Mack reminisced freely

about the early days of union organization in Twin Branch, Big Sandy, and the region I had known all my life.

While Mack has been unknown to folklorists, his brother Orville was a nationally recognized singer and writer of coal mining songs. These songs were a social history and commentary on unionization and the daily life of coal miners. During the interview, Mack produced some new material—songs, stories, and observations—previously unrecorded, on the development of UMWA strength in McDowell County as seen through the eyes of a union organizer.

As I prepared this interview for publication, I did not know that Mack Jenks died late in December of 1974. His brother Orville, also known as Jake, had died in New Mexico in the early 1960's.

J. Roderick Moore. I was talking to Orville's wife in Welch. She's just going back to Ohio. She said you used to sing with Orville at the union meetings and things.

Mack Jenkins. Yeah. Yeah, we made up any number of songs. Some of it we made together, and some of it he made a song and I made a song. And now, I have about maybe eight or nine that, well, there was one or two that he helped in and some he didn't. I don't know whether he put it on himself or whether he had some recording artist to

put it on, but he put on record the song about the little lump of coal.

RM Yes.

MJ And it's in Washington in the Library, at Washington, D.C., and it costs you $4.75 to get a record of it. I talked to his wife and she said, "I know that's your song and Jake didn't have nothing to do with it." See, it was my own composition. But he recorded it, or had it recorded. I don't know which, and had it put on record.

RM Well, when did you start singing together?

MJ Oh, all our lives. Me and him, we've sung together in churches. We'd sing together. He accompanied us with the guitar.

When we was young, right up here at Big Sandy and right here in this camp, too, he used to operate the harps all the time. I'd keep as many as four or five harps—different keys. And we would play for dances up here at Big Sandy. On Friday night they would let us have the theater after the show, and we'd just move the seats back and get all the room we wanted. Sometimes I've seen as many as 20 and 24 couples on the floor, square dancing. And, me and him, and one of my brother-in-laws and a boy by the name of Frost, one of the Frost boys out of Henson Hollow, we played music all the time for 'em to square dance. We'd start square dancing right after the show and be right there when broad daylight come the next morning.

RM Where did you all learn to play your instruments? Did you learn through your father?

MJ Naw, we just picked it up.

RM When did you all move down here to this area?

MJ We moved here in 1908.

RM How old were you and how old was Orville?

MJ I was eight and Orville was about ten. He's about two years older than I was.

RM Were you all playing instruments, playing music, at that time?

MJ No, no.

RM Just started down here, then?

MJ We mostly got together along in the '20's, the early '20's. I just picked up the harp playing, you know, and he did the same way about playing the guitar.

Well, now, he married into a family where he and the boys all played some kind of a string instrument. So he picked up playing the guitar. One of his wife's brothers, Jess, Jess Johnson—they called him "The Fiddlin' Fool." He was the best violin player in the state of West Virginia. And in fact he went, I don't know whether it was New York or not, but he got to playing in a big orchestra, playing second fiddle.

RM About what year did you and Orville start playing for dances and things around here?

MJ It was the early '20's.

RM Did you all play for right many dances before you started playing at union meetings?

MJ Yeah, because the union didn't come into here 'til 1933, the summer of 1933. That's when the union come in. And in fact we helped organize a lot. I don't know of Orville a-being into it, but I know I was. Gary Hollow—after these other places already had the local set up—Gary Hollow, we didn't have it organized. We had a tough time in Gary Hollow. And then you might have heard tell of a place over here, in the northern part of the field here, by the name of Widen. We had trouble at Widen. At that time I was at Otsego in Wyoming County. That was in '40 and '41. I was president of the Otsego local.

RM When you all were playing for dances and things back in the '20's, were you listening to many records or many other musicians?

MJ No, the only thing we heard then was these old-timey Victrolas.

RM Yeah, do you remember any of the people you used to listen to on the old Victrolas? What about Gid Tanner? Charlie Poole?

MJ No, I don't remember none of them. But old Grandpappy Jones, we've listened to him.

RM Tell me about the organizing.

MJ We'd have these big meetings, you know, and you'd have to go in there and sign a check-off card and leave it there. Well, we didn't have no locals at that time, but we signed these check-off cards and the union—head officials of the union—gets these check-off cards.

Well that's the way we had to do it in Gary. We would slip around up there in Gary and get men to sign these check-off cards. We'd get all that we could to sign these check-off cards. We'd have to go in the late hours of the night, because these here, what we called thugs, Baldwin-Felts men and state police, caught us up at Gary Hollow, ah, buddy, it was just too bad. You just paid off. And they'd kick you out of that hollow.

Old man Ciphers lived on a lease way up there in the head of Gary Hollow, No. 9 Gary. And we'd slip up there in the late hours of the night and take these check-off cards to him. He kept a record book, you see, and he'd put all these names and check-off cards.

I was working for Ford up there at Twin Branch in '33, and a merchant there in Davy, Milt Burgess, he paid for our charter. It cost $20 then to get a charter, you see, for a local union. And Milt Burgess, he paid the $20 for our charter. We didn't get to keep the charter very long because Ford at that time, he was paying far better money than the union was paying, and they wouldn't recognize the union.

We had a grievance there which we shouldn't have nothing to have done with at all. But, you know, there was always what we called rednecks, someone to stir up trouble all the time, always keeps trouble stirred up. They called us the bunch of men up there that shut Ford down, and it was shut down on my birthday.

I worked on the 16th day of January, of '34, and I came home that night. I lived in an apartment right there on the main street of Davy. Goodson's store let us have one room upstairs for a union hall, you see, and we had our meetings in there. And on the 16th night we had a call meeting at the union hall over this grievance. It was over the powerhouse, now, it wasn't concerning the miners, it was over the powerhouse.

RM Was that up there at the dam?

MJ Yeah. So we shut Ford down, and never did work no more, Ford didn't.

RM He didn't open up Twin Branch again?

MJ No. Well, he leased it out to other people, but he never did run no more at Twin.

RM Do you remember the first time that you and Orville sang at a union meeting?

MJ Well, I'll say it was in '33.

RM Do you remember where?

MJ Well, over here at Coney Island. Used to be there wasn't no business at all over there, when the area was organized in '33. There was any number of little tents made out of brattice cloth.

RM Coney Island. Would they advertise that you all were coming to sing at the meeting, or would you all just be there?

MJ No, no. We'd just get there. Now, then, I'll tell you what Orville did. In '35, the first convention of the United Mine Workers after this southern part of West Virginia was organized, they had the convention in Cincinnati, Ohio.

I had a brother that worked down near Iaeger, back this side of Iaeger, He was a checkwayman for the United Mine Workers. And at this convention they'd send so many delegates from each local. Well, he was elected a delegate down there to represent that local in the convention. Well, there was a special train, they stopped every so often. They stopped at Welch, they stopped at Iaeger, and they'd pick all these here delegates up.

Now, Orville, he lived at Hemphill in a hollow we called Slick Rock. He lived up Slick Rock Hollow. And he went out to Sherman's Pawn Shop there in Welch and bought him his guitar, a Gibson Second. It was a good guitar, but yet it wasn't the best that they made. And he said he went out there and caught that train that night. It run about the time No. 3 run, about 11 o'clock in the night. He went out there and bought him a ticket to Cincinnati and got on that train with his guitar and that bunch of delegates. And my [other] brother, then, he

Mack Jenks holding his grandson Charles Robert Stone about 1950. Photographer unknown.

got on down there at Iaeger.

Now, he went to Cincinnati with him and he said that all these meetings that they had at the convention, he was there. And any time there was a speaker come up, you know, to address the bunch of delegates, they'd always call him up to play for 'em. John L. Lewis was there. He had one song he called "The John L. Lewis Blues" and he said it just tickled old John L. to death to get him up there singing that. And he stayed there, he said, 14 days he was in Cincinnati. He said he attended every one of their meetings and all the big dinners they had, he was a guest at it. And he came back home and said he counted 270-some dollars, you know, where they'd take the hat around and they'd throw in and donate. And he said he made a lot more money on the trip. Said he slept in the very best bed, drink the very best liquor.

RM Did he ever stop working in the mines to play music?

MJ No.

RM How often did you play? You all played right often at the union meetings didn't you?

MJ Yeah

RM Maybe once a week?

MJ No, maybe it'd be once a month or maybe it'd go six months. Just whenever we got together. And whenever there'd be a dance, or anything like that, we'd play. That's all.

RM You say you wrote many of the songs also?

MJ Yeah, oh, yeah.

RM Who wrote "Dying Brakeman Blues?"

MJ Oh, I don't know as either one of us wrote that song. You're talkin' about "The Motorman Song."

RM Uh-huh, "The Motorman Song."

MJ Orville might have done it. I wouldn't say he didn't. But that happened right around here, not two miles from here—in the mines. Now that happened right around here.

I knowed the boy well. The boy's name

was Hiram Hall, that got killed. And the man that was runnin' the motor that killed him was Charlie Landrum. I broke for him a many day. And nipped for him a many day. As you know, a nipper takes care of the cable, you see—where the motor has to go where there ain't no trolley wire, he used a nip and a cable. There was a stirrup on the motor, the nipper has to stay in that stirrup. In case the cable hangs up he's got to get it loose, you see. And I've nipped for Charlie and I broke for him. He was a good motorman. But this boy got killed braking for Charlie. And that's what the song was made up of, and I don't know whether Orville made the song up or not. I know I didn't have nothing to do with it.

RM If Orville didn't, is there anyone else?

MJ Not as I know of.

RM Well, do you remember many of the songs that you all made up together and used to sing?

MJ Not too many that we made up together. But I have my own, and then I have some that we made up together.

RM Do you have those written down?

MJ No.

RM Do you remember them?

MJ Yeah, they're back up there.

RM Can you still sing them?

MJ Oh. yeah.

RM Would it be possible to get you to sing them?

MJ Oh, yes. That's what I told ya, I'd be glad to do it. Because you see, I'm old. If the Lord just give me one more year, you know, or one more day, I'm satisfied. I've had a long life. The 17th of this next month, I'll be 72 year old. And so I'd be glad to give 'em to you, let you do whatever you want to with 'em. And if you put 'em on record, that'd be perfectly all right.

Any number of songs that I've got—they're my own, just my own compositions. Now, "The Little Lump of Coal," he never put a word in that song. But yet, I was told he put it on record. I don't know, I never heard it, you see. That was my own composition.

RM One of his daughters said that he never wrote to music, he just wrote the words and used the music from other songs.

MJ Well, that's the way we did, you see. We just practiced up a tune and placed the words in it, such as "The Maple on the Hill." You know the song about "The Maple on the Hill?" Now, that is what "The Little Lump of Coal" is worded to, "The Maple on the Hill," you see.

RM Could you do the mining songs first?

MJ Oh, yeah. You want the mining songs?

RM Yeah, let's start with the mining songs if you could.

MJ (Sings "The Little Lump of Coal")·

I'm just a poor miner, boys, I labor for my bread.
This story in my memory I've heard told,
For the sake of wife and babies how a miner risks his life,
For the price of just one lump of coal.

Don't forget me, little darling, when they lay me down to rest.
Tell my brothers all these loving words I say.
Let the flowers be forgotten, sprinkle coal dust on my grave
In remembrance of the UMWA.

I used to be a motor runner not so many years ago,

Used to work the starting box and fight the pole.
Me and my good brakeman, we would scuffle all day long,
For the price of just one lump of coal.

Mother Jones is not forgotten by the miners to this field.
She has gone to rest above, God rest her soul;
She tried to march the boys to victory but was punished here in jail
For the price of just one little lump of coal.

Don't forget me little darlin', when they lay me down to rest.
Tell my brothers all these living words I say.
Let the flowers be forgotten, sprinkle coal dust on my grave
In remembrance of the UMWA.

RM That was great. That was good. And you wrote that?

MJ That's my own composition.

RM Do you remember what year you wrote it?

MJ Well I'd say it was in '34, about '34.

RM How did you come to write the song?

MJ I don't know. They just come in my mind. I'd just sit down and write 'em out. I know I wrote one sitting here one day babysitting for my wife's father.

RM Now, when you all would sing at a local meeting, would you sing at the beginning of the meeting or—?

MJ Oh, just anytime during the meeting. Maybe ahead of the speaker.

RM Were there many other people besides you and Orville that would perform at the meetings?

MJ No, not many. And union songs—there wasn't too many a-singing.

RM Well, did anybody ever write down any union songs that you all wrote?

MJ No. Not as I know of.

RM You always played the harp behind him?

MJ I led with the harp. He followed me with the guitar.

RM Did you all ever make up any songs that were sort of good-time songs or happy songs or anything?

MJ Oh, yes. We had some funny songs.

RM Do you remember any of those?

MJ Oh, yes. Yes

RM Well, could you sing one of those?

MJ Well, now—this is one I made up

about men that didn't like the union, you know. And we called them "scabs," and we'd get rid of them if we could. And one of the head men over here at the main office, his name was Jess Quinto. Then there was another field man by the name of Johnny Griegle. He's still over there at the field office. Then we had another field man whose name was Matthew Daison. Well, I made up a song about them. The title of the song is "The Union Blues." (singing)

There was a man name's Jess Quinto
Says the scabs will have to go
And build their local in the devil's den
Well, you get no easy chair, for the devil's boss down there.
You'll get just what is coming to you then.

For the devil and his wife, they keep no dry packed ice
To put around your feet if they get hot.
Well, they're not the least bit slow, for they're always on the go.
And they sure do keep the snitchers on the trot.

Both sides of a matchbook advertising Jenks' unsuccessful candidacy in the 1952 primary election for justice of the peace.

For I cannot like a fellow, that seems the
    least bit yellow,
And does not like to pay his union dues.
Well, we ought to cut some slab, right in
    on these here scabs,
And whip 'em 'til they'll take the union
    blues.

For a man named Johnny Griegle,
He's not the least bit fickle
And would not laugh at any man's
    downfall,
But I'm sure that Matthew Daison
Would bust his sides a-laughin',
If we would take a stick and kill 'em all.

But I cannot like a fellow, that seems the
    least bit yellow,
And does not like to pay his union dues.
Well, we ought to cut some slabs, right
    in on these here scabs,
And whip 'em 'til they'll take the union
    blues.
I mean to tell you.
To whip 'em 'til they'll take the union
    blues.

RM When did you write that?
MJ (laughs) Back in '36 or '38, longer than that.
RM And you wrote that all yourself?
MJ Yeah, that's mine.
RM And what was the name of it?
MJ "The Union Blues."
RM "The Union Blues," and what was the tune behind it?
MJ I don't know. (laughs)
RM O.K.
MJ I just whipped up a tune. Put the words to it.
RM Well, could you do the funeral song that the union asked you and your brother to write?
MJ Yeah, let's see.
RM What is the name of that? Is it called "Only A Miner?"
MJ Yeah, "Only A Miner" is the title of it. (singing)

Well a miner has gone to make heaven
    his home,
His wife and dear children he left here
    alone.
Let men of the union, from this rank
    and file
Put an arm of protection around this
    dear child.

He is only a miner, was killed
    underground.
He is only a miner, and one more is
    gone.
Why he was taken, nobody can tell.
His mining is over — poor miner,
    farewell.

He leaves his companion and little
    ones too, .
To earn their own living as all miners do,
Shut off from daylight and those that
    he loves.
The boulder that crushed him came
    down from above.

He is only a miner, was killed
    underground.
He is only a miner, and one more is gone.
Why he was taken, nobody can tell.
His mining is over — poor miner,
    farewell.
His mining is over — dear brother,
    farewell.

RM Did you all sing that very much?
MJ No, no. After we sung that at the local hall, and they said "Buddy, we don't want no part of that." We just dismissed it. Of course, it's still stuck in my memory.

RM When did you stop working in the mines?
MJ I stopped working there on April 2, 1959.
RM Where was the last mine that you worked in?
MJ Over here on the Coalwood Road. The mines went right under the road.
RM I guess you started just the small punch mines, didn't you?
MJ No, I started in a large mine about two miles — no, it's not two miles up the road here. Hensley. I was a boy when I first started to work. Now, there was a large family of us — it's 12. And I started work when I was a boy 12 years old. I worked the summer that I was 12 years, and my name was put on the company payroll. I got seven and a half cents an hour, worked ten long hours a day for 75 cents.
RM What did you do?
MJ I knocked latches on a tipple, where they dropped the cars over the hill with a rope, and they would dump and you had to go knock a latch to let the door swing out for the coal to come down through the bottom. Then I went to school part of the winter that winter. And when a boy was 13 years old he would go and make a sworn affidavit before a notary public that they would not sue the workman's compensation in case you got killed. Then they'd let you work in the mines. I was 13 years old, on the 17th day of January, and in March, the following March of that same year, I went inside the mines. And I got a dollar and a quarter a day, 12 and a half cents a hour for labor inside. And I have been in the mines up until '59. I've been about 44 years inside of 'em. Some of 'em coal was 28 inches high. You'd had to hunt a place where the top had fell out before you could even turn up the thermos bottle and get all the coffee out of it.
RM Well, I think they said Orville wrote a song called "White House Blues." Do you remember that?
MJ No, but I remember him *havin'* the "White House Blues," and then he had the "John L. Lewis Blues."
RM What about a song about a Model T?
MJ No . . . but he had one about all the different kinds of tobaccos.
RM He did?
MJ Yeah.

I saw his mother stand beside him,
Saw the tears stream down her face
As she prayed to God the Father —
Must he die here in this place?
As she prayed to God the Father,
She said, Father, you know best.
If my darling boy is dying,
Father take him home to rest.
Yes, Father, take him home to rest.

MJ Now that was the words of "The Dying Coupler," some call it "The Motorman."

RM Well, you seem to think that Orville might not have written that?

MJ Well, I don't know, now. I'll just be honest with you, I couldn't say whether Orville wrote that song or not.

RM Were there other songs like that during that time?

MJ No. I never knowed none like that. Now, me and him would sing it together, you see. I believe it's much better where there's two a-singing it together, you see, because they can fill in with other words besides what just the lead man is giving out.

RM Well, do you think you might remember some more songs about the mines that you wrote?

MJ Well, now, I had one about the Bartley explosion, but I've forgot some of it. It was sung to the tune of "One Step More." You've heard the old song "For It's Only One Step More?" It was sung to that. Now that happened in 1940, when Bartley Mine blowed up over on Dry Fork and killed 91. I had a song on that but now I studied here for the last month trying to get that song back together because I knew you was coming, and I tried to get that song back together and I never have been able to get it back together.

RM Could you sing what you do have together?

MJ Yeah

RM I'd like to, you know, have some record of it at least.

MJ Well, it was made up about the Bartley explosion. (singing)

In the year of 1940, on the 10th day
of the year,
There was a bunch of poor coal
·miners
Left there loved ones, sweet and dear.

RM Do you remember any of those?

MJ No, I don't remember; I couldn't begin to sing that. Now, did we get that motorman song on there for you?

RM No, do you know that?

MJ Yeah.

RM Would you sing that for us?

MJ Yeah boy, sure would. Now that happened; that was a true happening. I knowed the boy that was braking—a boy by the name of Hiram Hall; and I knowed the motorman that he was braking after, Charlie Landrum was the man who was running the motor. (singing)

See that brave and trembling motorman
Who says his age is twenty-one.
See him stepping from his motor,
Crying, Lord, what have I done?
Have I killed my brave young coupler,
Is it so that he is dyin'?
Lord, I tried to stop the motor
But I could not stop in time.

I saw the car wheels rolling o'er him,
Saw them bend his weary head.
I saw his sister stoop and kiss him,
Crying, brother, are you dead?
Yes, I'm dying, sister, dying,
Soon I'll reach that blissful shore
There to join with friends and loved ones
For my coupling days are o'er.

Oh a miner's life's not easy,
You can see what happened there.
They were entombed beneath the
    mountain
Without the slightest breath of air.
Oh, these men, these poor coal
    miners,
Oh, their work on earth is o'er.
They are now at rest with Jesus
Over on the other shore.

RM You all sang at the union meetings; was there ever any singing in the mines?

MJ In the mines? Yes, they's plenty of singing in the mines. Orville, I broke for him months in and months out, and many times when we'd have to go a long trip with a motor and string of cars, I've sat on the bumper and him in the deck of the motor and we'd sing together. We'd sing different songs, most always religious songs. And he could put in a good alto and we'd sing together.

RM Were there many other men that sang in the mines also?

MJ No, no. You can prob'ly hear some fellow singing of his work, and that's all.

RM But you all did sing some in the mines?

MJ Yeah, we sung together a lot, but that would be the time we'd be a-traveling a right smart distance with a triple car, and I'd be setting on the bumper with him.

RM Well, did you both start singing in a church originally?

MJ Well no, no. Now, I been down in Ohio where he lived down there, and I'd go to church with him, and we'd most always sing a song or two there in church.

RM I just wondered when you were young, if that's where you started singing together?

MJ No. We was up in our years. We didn't do much singin' in the 20's you see. We just played music and mostly for those square dances, but when we started singing together was in the '30's.

RM Well, did you write very much music when you all were playing for the square dances?

MJ No.

RM You just played somebody else's music, then?

MJ Yeah. The old-timey songs.

RM And it wasn't until you started in the mines, then, the union, that you all started making up songs?

MJ That's right. After the union come in, we started making up songs to sing at the local union and at these big gatherings that they have. You know they always have a John L. Lewis Day somewhere, and we'd usually be at them and sing.

RM Would you all try to write a new

song for each big gathering or each new John L. Lewis Day?

MJ No. We just put on what we had, for them songs just come to you now and then.

RM Well, they used to have a lot of entertainers come in for the John L. Lewis Days, didn't they?

MJ Oh, Law', yeah. That's a big day through this part of the country. 'Course, it's not like it was ten or 15 years ago. It's just like everything else, you see, it just eventually wears away.

John L. and FDR on the Mantel

Family Life After Unionization

■ BY BIRDIE BLEDSOE KYLE

Birdie Bledsoe Kyle grew up on Cabin Creek in the 1940's, after the union was firmly established there. She remembers plenty of hard work and a tight family budget, but none of the bitter hopelessness that older people recall from the nonunion era. Perhaps most dramatic was the sense of empowerment that unionization brought to mining families, represented in the Bledsoe household by portraits of John L. Lewis and Franklin D. Roosevelt on the mantel of their coal company house.

Kyle's first-hand account was published in the April–June 1980 GOLDENSEAL.

Birdie Kyle, a Congressional aide, worked for Senator Jennings Randolph when she wrote this account.

I am a native West Virginian, born in Fayette County at MacDunn, but raised up on Cabin Creek in the coalfields, from the age of ten—my father left Koppers Coal Company and went to work for Truax Traer in 1945. My truest memories, then, are of Cabin Creek's coal towns—not of Fayette County—but I have a picture of myself sitting on the bottom step (at one year old of the house in which I was born, a one-room abandoned boxcar. When I was little, my older sister tormented me when she felt like it by calling me "old Boxcar Bill." I don't remember which made me the maddest—being reminded that I was born in a boxcar, or being called "Bill" when I was a *girl*! Probably both.

How I remember the mixed feelings we had about coal company scrip. If you went down to the coal company store to purchase groceries, you "drew" scrip. If you needed "dry goods" you charged them—and those charges along with whatever scrip you "drew" were taken out of Dad's pay on payday. Many times my father picked up an empty envelope trying to feed 12 children and clothe them—we "drew" a lot of scrip, I can tell you. Scrip could make you schizophrenic. You had to decide between two evils: drawing scrip and having no cash on hand—or not drawing scrip so that Dad could draw a payday, by trying to stretch the groceries and home-canned food in the meantime. Usually, our family, due to its size, lost the scrip battle.

I do recall, though, that you could draw a $2 bill—but I don't think you could do it daily, perhaps only once a week. That $2 was expected to do a lot of things it couldn't do even then—it couldn't pay for school lunches for 12 children, and take everyone to a movie once a week, even if the fare was only 15 cents (and it was). Of course, we could have packed our lunches; but "light bread" was too expensive to purchase in the quantities needed to pack 12 lunches, and we were too proud to pack a biscuit sandwich. (Now, of course, biscuits are a treat, and we would be proud to take a biscuit sandwich anywhere any time.) My Mom tried to save the $2 in cash so she could pay for our school books (oh, yes, they had to be bought back then—in cash). But books were mandatory at our house—school books and encyclopedias, no comics. The Bible, of course, was very acceptable reading

material.

The tipple was every bit as dominant in the coalfields as the company store. I can see the chute leading up the mountain towards the men who were (in my day) hand-loading coal that would shoot downward to the tipple and into the waiting jaws of the ever present black coal cars, raising huge clouds of "bug dust" that wafted in every direction and settled on everything—including my mother's newly washed starched curtains drying on the curtain stretchers on the front porch. Lord, how we washed those curtains and those windows.

The coal cars, full of coal, sat on the sidetrack, being switched further away from the tipple to make room for more. Finally, late at night, the engines came (steam, not diesel) and switched the cars back and forth along the sidetrack away from the main railroad line.

All night long the hissing and clanking of coupling and uncoupling coal cars kept you company if you were awake in the dark—but it didn't scare you. It made you comfortable, because you knew that along with that engine and those coal cars, came humans, real people, and they were out there in the dark, calling to one another and laughing. You knew they'd watch out for you and keep away monsters and ghosts (and this was especially comforting to a little girl whose older brother and sister had regaled her with graveyard stories just before bedtime). I used to feel really sad when finally the loaded cars were all hooked together and the engine was at the front, the red caboose I knew was on the end, and the steam engine whistle blew as it entered the main rail line and took the coal away.

Next morning when it was light, there as if a miracle had happened, were empty cars waiting to be filled with the coal my father, and other fathers, sons and brothers, loaded by hand and sent down the mountain.

Pictures remind me of the miners in their work gear, and the little carbide lamp attached to their hard hats—and we loved to help put carbide in the little pop-top hole in the bronze lamp that would light Daddy's way down in the mine. And we knew our mother had put an extra "treat" into the lunch bucket so Daddy could "bring us something" from work. But that was only for little ones—and you never knew quite whether to be proud, or sad when you out-

grew being "little" enough to get a treat from the lunch bucket. Even then, the treat had a funny taste, and really wasn't that good; that wasn't the point. Daddy had gone down in the dark mines that morning, and the treat was proof positive that he had returned.

We were not unaware of that terrible wailing sound of the tipple whistle when a mine disaster had occurred. Even community grade schools turned out and headed for the tipple to wait for the man-trip to come down that little track from the top—carrying the miners who always "came out" when an accident occurred, if it was fatal. One knew, if one's Daddy didn't get off that final run, it must be him that got hurt or killed. Or, with shining hope, we would then tell one another that Daddy had stayed behind to help—and it was true every time for me. Because my father was never killed *in* the mines; he died six years ago of black lung. But many of my friends and neighbors watched and waited for one who never came—not, at least, climbing off that man-trip bringing the live ones out and down.

I remember those drafty old houses with their splintered floors, where the linoleum didn't quite reach far enough, and how cold they were in winter. It's true that only those standing right in front of those coal burning grates were warm, and then only one side at a time. I've built many a coal fire in those grates in each room of the house except the kitchen.

Ah, the kitchen stove was a wonder—it had a tank on the side that heated the water for the returning miner's bath before dinner. Each of us children (of the 12—10 girls and two boys) had to take turns getting up each winter morning and "building the fires"—kitchen having first priority since it takes a good hot oven to bake bread every morning. My older brother told me that if I'd slip outside, across the narrow dirt road, and into the sidetrack where the coal cars waited, and if I'd lift the trap on the "dope boxes" on those cars and grab a handful of "dope" (I don't know the real name for "dope," and I don't know why it was there)—but if I'd do that, and bring the dope back to the kitchen stove, its greenish slick cottony bulk would burn like mad and start that kitchen kindling and coal to burning in no time. He was right. He cautioned me not to get caught, or I'd surely land in jail. It was a long time before I figured out he was probably kidding about jail.

Imagine a family of 14 in various stages of growth and noise, living in a coal company house of four rooms, one of them the kitchen, and you will imagine wall-to-wall double beds, and you won't be wrong. You had to have a lot of seniority to get a "big" house, big enough to accommodate a large family. It was cozy in winter, though. All the houses had front and back porches. We sat out there in summer, and our mother would build "gnat smokes" to keep the bugs away. It worked, too. I wonder how many readers remember how to build a gnat smoke?

I remember John L. Lewis; we had a picture of him framed, on the mantel (all coal company houses had mantels over the fireplace grates). Beside his picture, also framed, was FDR. I grew mighty tall before I figured out they weren't respected relatives on whom we could depend for better times, but respected and revered leaders—one of the coal miners' union and the other of a desperate nation. But I loved to listen to the sound of their voices on the radio—and if we didn't care to listen, we had better be quiet because it was tantamount to treason to make a noise during those fireside chats that might cause one to miss a single word of what was being said.

I remember my first day of school (and yes, it's true we walked miles to school in those days, snow or shine), but what makes my first day of school memorable is the total, devastating disappointment! Somehow I had come to believe that if Franklin Roosevelt, a household word, was the great-est man in the world, and if the second greatest segment of humanity were, as I was led to believe, teachers, then it was reasonable to expect that Eleanor Roosevelt would be the teacher. She wasn't. I cried. The new teacher understood, and at the end of my first day, I was certain I did not care that much; my teacher was nice, and she gave me a ride home so I wouldn't have to walk. I backslid only once on the way home, thinking how much more exciting it would be to arrive home in teacher's car if teacher was Eleanor! I was a celebrity, nonetheless, and soon forget my longing for Mrs. Roosevelt.

Children are impressionable—and my whole life and that of my family during my "formative" years revolved around John L. Lewis and Franklin Roosevelt. Those are my earliest and clearest memories.

Growing Up on Cabin Creek

An Interview with Arnold Miller

■ BY MICHAEL KLINE. ■ PHOTOGRAPHS BY RICK LEE

While coal miners fought to build their union, John L. Lewis built his own dictatorial machine to control it. Iron rule served the United Mine Workers of America reasonably well during the presidency of Lewis himself, a brilliant leader venerated by his membership. But the faulty legacy of the Lewis years became quickly apparent when he left the union to corrupt henchmen nurtured under his regime. Thus the final culmination of the fight for labor democracy came decades after the Mine Wars, as southern West Virginians joined their union brothers in a struggle to reform the UMWA. Ironically, the national leader that emerged to carry them to victory in 1972 was Arnold Miller, a son of Cabin Creek in the heart of the old Mine Wars country.

This 1981 interview discusses Miller's formative years in a community saturated with Mine Wars lore, bringing him to the eve of the union reform era.

When I first knew Arnold Miller some ten years ago he was involved in an awesome campaign for the presidency of the United Mine Workers of America, against the entrenched establishment of Tony Boyle. In those days, if you could get a word with Arnold, it usually had to do with some strategic detail of the hectic race. But I caught enough sketchy anecdotes about his past to realize that his life had been forged in struggle, that this controversial would-be president was in many ways the embodiment of coalfield experience, and I resolved to find time someday to hear the whole story.

When I visited with Mr. Miller at his apartment on Ruffner Avenue in Charleston last September I found him relaxed and reflective. We spent a whole afternoon talking about his early life, and I asked him to concentrate on those details of the story which preceded his presidency. Excerpts from that taped interview have been pulled together in this article.

Arnold Miller was born in Leewood, on Cabin Creek in Kanawha County, on April 25, 1923, just two years after The Battle of Blair Mountain, which broke the union effort in southern West Virginia until 1933. But union spirit and determination ran deep in his family psyche on both sides. He began by telling about his father.

Arnold Miller. My daddy was born in Bell County, in Pineville in east Kentucky, and was forced to migrate out of Kentucky to West Virginia at the age of 14, ostensibly for his organizing activity. He was a veteran miner at the age of 14, had five years in the mines. It's not common for people to understand today that years ago they worked children in the mines. I had a group picture I could show you somewhere here in Charleston. Showed about 30 miners, only two of which were adults. It's obvious from looking at the picture that children did work in the mines in the early days. They worked them like

slaves. They didn't pay them but damn little, and they dogged them around. Mining is far different today than it was then.

Michael Kline. Did your daddy come from a big family?

AM Yes. I believe there was 12 in the family. I don't know exactly the breakdown of boys and girls. I have one uncle and three aunts still living, and the rest of the family on my dad's side is about all gone.

MK What was your dad's dad's name?

AM John Miller. He had been a coal miner some in his younger days. He was primarily a farmer and didn't work that much around the mines.

MK Do you suppose your granddad was in a hard way? Why do you think he would let a nine-year-old son go in the coal mines?

AM I don't think there was any work hardly at all except in the mines itself. Particularly in that part of Kentucky where my family was raised. And conditions was

Arnold Miller in front of the coal storage silos at the Bethlehem Mines preparation plant at Kayford.

so tough then that everyone in the family that was able had to work in order to make ends meet. Far different than it is today, 'cause the wages even in the mines didn't pay much then. I believe my father when he went to work in the mines got 75¢ a day for trapping. They didn't pay a lot more than that for full-time adults. My dad opened and closed doors on the haulage way to direct air to the work faces. They had what you called airlocks. You opened one door for the haulage motor to get in, then you opened the other one for it to get out on the other side. You'd keep the circulation of air going to the working faces, to prevent such things as explosions and to keep the air at the proper level so that the men would be able to work.

MK Do you know where your granddaddy Miller came from?

AM Oh, yes, the family came from a little town called Hummel in Germany, my great-granddad and three brothers. They settled in east Kentucky. I think perhaps my grandfather, too, was born in the old country. He lived till he was 96, and he's not been dead all that many years. The Miller family was raised religiously in the Dunkard belief that adhered strictly to the Bible as it was written.

I remember my grandfather Miller in his later years owned some property in Fayette County and it was a problem for my dad and my uncles to keep him from trying to work when he was up in 80 years of age. He believed in working, and he didn't believe in using modern conveniences. He thought very little of walking 15, 20 miles a day, and often as not we would miss him. We'd go around and check on the land he owned, and generally found him farming somewhere—it wasn't like gardening.

One time we visited him and he had about two acres of half-runner beans out,

and I asked him, said, "Dad, what are you going to do with all those beans?" He said, "Well, I'll sell some and give the rest away, there's nothing wrong with giving them away as long as I find somebody that needs them." And that's the way he was. He had to be out growing or he had to be out working. He was up in the 80's before we finally stopped him from working at the sawmill. He worked in the timber quite a lot.

One time when I was visiting one of my uncles, granddad come in one winter day. His overalls, when he took 'em off you could stand 'em in the corner. They was froze well above his knees. And while he was getting a bath we gathered 'em all up and burnt 'em. When he come out of the bath, the first thing he done is opened the cap on the stove—old coal burning stove—and looked in and saw the remnants of the overalls, the buckles and so forth.

"By shuckings," he said, "you boys have burned up my work clothes! Now I'll have to go buy some more." We had a dickens of a time getting him to realize we didn't want him working. He didn't have to work. And we finally got him to quit. But he would go out and put in the crops if we didn't watch him real close.

MK So your dad went to work in the coal mines when he was nine, and by the time he was 14 he was in trouble for organizing?

AM Yes. He was driven out of Kentucky because of his organizing activity.

MK So how did your dad get to Cabin Creek?

AM Back in those days, when you looked for employment, you would look for word-of-mouth information on where someone was hiring. They'd go wherever there was some hope for work. Most of the mines in the area of Cabin Creek when I grew up didn't work much at all in the winter time. Generally they worked one day a week and they'd have what was referred to by the miners as "block-up day." That meant you could go out to the mines and work if you wanted to, shoot down your coal, timber up your place—it was all hand-loading then—and get your work place in a condition where, when the mine did work, you might load another car or two of coal and make perhaps a dollar or two more when the mines did work. But your were not paid for working on a "block-up day." In fact, a lot of days you'd go out, and if you shot any powder you paid for it yourself.

My dad worked in the Cabin Creek area back in the early days, around 1920. And when the union was broke in 1921 my dad

and my granddad on my mother's side had to leave Cabin Creek and go find work elsewhere. They were driven off Cabin Creek and took employment in this little town called Leewood. My dad did not come back. That's when my mother and dad separated, and my dad worked in Fayette County for a number of years in Ansted for the Gauley Mountain Coal Company. He subsequently became president of the Ansted local, and was president there until that operation shut down.

My mother's name was Lula Burgess Hoy, and my mother's dad was Joseph Hoy. They came to Cabin Creek in 1903.

MK So he must have been there during the labor wars of 1912, '13?

AM In 1912 my granddad was president of his local union on Cabin Creek and the customary practice in those days, when they wanted you to leave, the coal company would order you to get in the creek and dare you to get out till you got to the mouth of Cabin Creek. But because he

was a very honest individual, my grand-dad was not asked to "hit the creek," but was given the opportunity to move some of his belongings. He later returned. He was president of one of the early local unions on Cabin Creek.

MK Your grandfather was a well-educated man, did you tell me?

AM My grandfather Hoy had a total of two months schooling in his entire lifetime. But he could read and write, figure with anyone in the country, and he was smarter politically than anyone I've ever run into before or since. Sometimes I didn't agree with his political philosophy. But it's history today, and what he said to me then always proved to be true.

He wasn't much of a talker, so it made it easier to remember the things he said. Where I didn't follow his advice I found later he was correct. I remember when I was growing up he said, "Son, we all come into this world equal, but there's a hell of a lot of people that don't understand that, they don't believe it." His political philosophy was that the Democratic party was the only one that ever done anything for the working class of people. I feel that's true yet today.

I lived through three Republican administrations. I don't remember them ever doing anything for the working class of people. I was raised in the Hoover days, and an old Republican asked me one time,

"Why are you a Democrat?" I said, "Hoover made a Democrat out of me." He thought for a moment or two and then said, "Young man, I remember you from the day you come into this world. You wasn't old enough to work in the Hoover days." I said, "No, sir. But I was old enough to eat!" I remember the slogans that were cast about in those days: "A chicken in every pot and two cars in every garage." None of which was true.

MK Might have been true for the coal operators.

AM Well, they was the only ones that ate. I remember going to the company store and they had a meat case. We looked, but we did not buy anything in the meat case. The meat case was only for the operators themselves.

They talk about prices today. Why, prices were much higher then, in the Hoover days, than they are today. The wages were so pitifully low, you can understand why the miner did not buy anything at the meat counter. It was tough for a miner to make $2.00 a day in those days. And such extras as pork chops would cost you about $2.00 a pound in those days. So we only looked. I was 14 years old before I knew a hog had anything but sow belly! We were lucky if we got a small piece of fatback to put in the greens.

MK Your family kept a garden though, didn't they?

AM Oh, yes, I remember the hillsides on Cabin Creek in those days were skinned up almost two-thirds of the way up the hill on both sides of the holler going up, and they were gardened. You gardened in those days or you didn't eat, it was just that simple.

There were no social programs in those days, no nothing. If a man was injured in the mine in Leewood, where I was born and raised, the only hope for him getting any kind of medical help was to be hauled in a wagon 12 miles down Cabin Creek. I heard my mother say one time that if the injury didn't kill a man the wagon ride would. She talked about women and children dying from what we refer to as common ailments today, appendicitis, pneumonia, and such diseases as that. A lot of miners in those days suffered back fractures and they'd go home without the benefit of casts or anything else. They were left to their own device, to lay in bed at home and hopefully recover. That's why you see a lot of older miners who were injured in those days bent over and hardly able to walk. They simply were not very well taken care of.

When there was a big roof fall in the mine, the first question asked by the bosses, "Did any mules get hurt?" They thought more of the mule than they did the human being. They had to buy a mule, but they could hire another man. Not long after I first went to work I was told by the mine foreman, "If you don't like your damned job, get your cottonpicker over the hill. They's 200 living down there at the foot of the hill on a box of crackers and a can of sardines would like to have your job if you don't want it." It was tough to take that kind of criticism back in those days.

MK Why did the miners take it? Were there a lot of gun thugs on Cabin Creek in those days?

AM At that particular time the gun thugs outnumbered the miners three to one. And talking about the Baldwin-Felts thugs! No one needs to tell me what they were or how they operated. I saw the experience there. Miners were not allowed to congregate. Nowhere. If they saw a couple or three miners along the railroad track somewhere talking, the thugs—be three or four of them together—would approach them and start insulting them. They'd beat them till they couldn't get up. You might wonder why the miners didn't resist that, or maybe take a gun to them. The operators had prior to that declared martial law and took all the guns that the miners had. They had nothing to fight with. And the law was with the thugs, they were the law. It was unbearable. You hear people today talk about Constitutional rights! The man that worked in the mines in those days had no rights whatsoever, Constitutional or otherwise. It was nothing more than slavery.

Martial law was declared many times

The railroad linked Leewood to other towns, including Eskdale, with its independent merchants. "Being a gun nut from an early age, if I got 15¢, enough to buy a box of .22 shorts, I'd hit the railroad berm for Eskdale," Miller says. "A box of shells was more important to me than a movie."

during the labor wars. I don't remember all the specific dates; it seems to me like the last time they declared martial law on Cabin Creek was in 1927. I remember asking my granddad when I saw the militia come through with the old World War I wrap leggings and the little old flat dinky tin helmets. He said, "Tinhorns, son." That's what they were called in those days, tinhorns. And when I asked him what tinhorns were he gave me the perfect definition of a damn thug, which is actually what they were.

When the union came back in 1933, the Baldwin-Felts thugs that had any sense at all promptly left the coalfields. The ones that didn't were generally found shot down on their doorsteps. The miners had such a hatred for them that they eliminated as many of them as they could.

MK Did your granddad Hoy and your father ever have any dealings with Mother Jones, did they ever see her or hear her speak?

AM Oh, yes, Mother Jones was active in the Cabin Creek area. I don't remember exactly the last time. An old Syrian, Kabel Shibley, that lived on Cabin Creek from 1903 until his death a couple of years ago, showed me a picture of a rally that Mother Jones held. A little town called Eskdale was a mile below where I lived on Cabin Creek. She conducted this rally on the church porch there in Lamont Hollow, and you could see the militia in this picture parading up and down the railroad tracks.

The militia, National Guard, and everyone else told Mother Jones not to come in the area and conduct a rally. She walked up this holler and the machine gunners challenged her not to take one more step. She walked up to the machine gun, turned it over on the guys that were manning it, and called them all kinds of foul names and told them they didn't have the guts to pull the trigger, that she was going to conduct a rally there whether they liked it or not. And she did. She was a fearless woman.

She gave the miners enough courage that when she appeared in the coalfields to hold a rally, they would attend. You couldn't keep 'em from coming in. They defied the thugs and the so-called law and everything else, the coal operators.

MK Why didn't the thugs just gun her down?

AM I think because they were afraid of what might happen. She had such a following among the mine workers. They probably figured that would trigger an uprising. Even though they mistreated the miners as much as they could, they were still scared of them. Once you've got a miner to the breaking point, where he no longer has any fear at all, then you was in big trouble.

MK Tell me a little bit about your early childhood.

AM I grew up in a little town called Leewood, and what little education I got, I got it there. They had an elementary and junior high school in the same town, joined buildings. Today they've been torn down. I got nine years of schooling, or the equivalent of nine years. I managed to jump a couple of grades and finished up in seven years.

MK Were they company-run schools?

AM They were not company-run, but the schools were dominated by company influence in those days. They run everything. They run the banks, the schools, the government, and everything else.

MK What effect did they have on the schools?

AM They affected the kind of teachers you had. And they tried to project into the schools their way of thinking, politically as well as educational. There was a defiance of them trying to dictate their policies, but it was on a fragmented basis. There was no organized resistance against them at that time.

MK There was one area of your life that they didn't dominate, though, and that was your love of woods and . . .

AM When I became about five years old the only form of recreation we had in the coal camps was hunting and fishing. I had a profound love of the outdoors and I spent as much time as I possibly could in the woods as a child. An old fellow named Luther Snodgrass began taking me in the woods when I was five. He probably taught me as much as I know about woodcraft, taught me how to course bees, how to hunt and fish. He was a constant companion and I spent as much time as I could with him.

MK Was he something like a father to you?

AM Well, he was. He provided an opportunity for me to get out into the woods when my grandfather was crippled and wasn't able to go. I didn't realize until later how much respect I should have for him doing that, because I must have been some part of a bother to him at the age of five. But he had the patience to work with me and teach me as much as he could.

MK You told me your mother was a woman who meant what she said.

AM Yeah, they were much more stern in those days! They didn't spare the rod. I remember when I was growing up that on eight or ten occasions I got the hide ripped off of me unjustly. I was somewhat bitter about it, but as I got older I began to think: well, I got the hide peeled off me eight or ten times for things I didn't do, but there must have been eight or ten times when I deserved to get the hide peeled off me that I didn't get caught. So they sort of cancelled out. I respect the way I was raised and I respect the fact that I was poor, because whatever I accomplished in life I remembered where I come from. One of the greatest things a human being can remember is where you come from.

Leewood was a typical coal mining town. The mine that was there when I grew up employed 356 men. At that time they all lived in town: it was customary practice in those days. Today miners live all over the country. Some drive 50, 60 miles to work. But when I grew up they all lived in the town where the mine was. Part of that was because when you went to a place like that to get a job the company would tell you, "We'll give you a job, but you got to live in one of our houses and you got to deal in the company store." And that's just the way it was.

People were very much closer together then. All the problems that people had in the town of Leewood where I was born and raised were all the people's problems. They kind of stuck together. When I was seven or eight years old I remember asking an older miner, "How you getting along?" He says, "Son, I have poor ways and lots of them." And I've thought about that many times since then. It was true. People we much closer-knit then. And they got along much better, because if you didn't look to your neighbor for help, there was no place

"An old fellow named Luther Snodgrass began taking me in the woods when I was five. He taught me as much as I know about wood-craft, how to course bees, how to hunt and fish. I didn't realize until later how much respect I should have had for him, because I must have been some part of a bother."

else to look.

MK So from your very first memories, the union was more that just an organization, it was made up of people who . . .

AM The union, when it came back in '33, was such a blessing to the miners. When Franklin D. Roosevelt was elected in '32 our neighbor whooped and hollered all night long. He was so hoarse the next morning he couldn't talk. I asked him, "Mr. Cooley, what does the election of FDR mean to the coal miners?" He said, "It means we'll be able to organize!" I lived to see what he meant about Roosevelt. In '33 the miners were given the right to organize. As fast as you could get a meeting together, you had a union organized there. I've seen them fight over who was going to be first.

The union was helpful to the industry itself. They'd become so cutthroat that when the union came back in, it stabilized labor costs which helped to guarantee a profit. Why the operators hated the union so fiercely as they did will always be beyond my comprehension, 'cause the union was good for them also.

What I learned from my childhood days growing up in the coalfields was I acquired a distinct hatred for the operators themselves. They dominated everything that the miners could think about. They had the so-called company towns, the company stores, and you [were forced] to spend the greater part of your earnings with the company or you was booted off the job.

MK Was there a movie theater, or . . . ?

AM No, the nearest movie theater was in Eskdale, about a mile or two below there. That's where I saw my first movie, *Scarface*. It was a gangster movie. If we cold garner 10¢ for the movie ticket, we'd run down the railroad berm to the next town. That's where most of the individual merchants were also. Being a gun nut from an early age, if I got 15¢, enough to buy a box of shorts was more important to me than a movie, so I only went to the movie when I had enough for the shorts and a movie ticket both. That took 25¢, which was harder than hell to come by in those days.

I'd run errands for the miners' wives that lived in the company houses there and dealt in the company stores. Many times they would want to mail a letter; 3¢ then was the price of a stamp, and they would say to me, "See if you can get me 3¢ of mainline money." Mainline money was money itself. Otherwise it was scrip. Sometimes the miners would trade a dollar of scrip for 75¢ of mainline money. There were those that preyed on the miners in that respect.

MK What were some of your other memories? Did you have a ball team, or other recreation?

AM Every coal mining community then had a baseball team. Very competitive. You went to the nearest towns around to play a ball game. It was a common practice, if you beat 'em on the field you had to whip 'em, too. Sometimes they'd beat you and whip you, too. So there were a lot of battles.

We did a lot of battling when I was growing up, in the neighborhood, in the taverns, or wherever. They were generally straight-on confrontations, when you had a fist fight. But along about the mid-1940's, it got to where they'd bring into play knives and guns and everything. It got to be very dangerous. I've seen a lot of fist fights in taverns, but once it's over with they'd shake hands, go drink more beer, and later on maybe the same two'd fight again. But there wasn't so much grudges kept in those day. The miners themselves were very tough physically. The nature of the work itself, I guess, produced that.

MK What about courting? Who did the miners court, and who'd they marry? Just girls from the same camp?

AM Well, they generally would stray away from the camp where they was raised. They'd go wherever the women, the girls, would congregate. It was common practice for us in those days to come out on the river. The towns were bigger, had more girls. There was a kind of intrusion on the part of the Cabin Creek miners in those towns. Our boys would gang up and the town's people resented that, which brought on more fisticuffs, more fights.

I got involved in a lot of it because I went to the places where most of the girls hung out. And if I found one of them that wasn't married, you know, I would immediately make the effort to secure a date. I didn't give a damn whether they liked it or not, if she wasn't married then she's fair game. Some went even farther than that, had no qualms about taking on a married woman, which caused a lot more friction. The fights were more violent, there was a lot more shoot-outs in those days. When a place got the reputation that you were likely to get shot or cut, the weaker ones stayed away. But not the ones that didn't give a damn. I guess I was somewhere in between.

I finished what schooling I got by the time I was 14. I wasn't big enough then to work in the mines. They had an age limit then, but the criteria was if you was big enough. So I worked in the timber a couple of years, and then I went to the mine superintendent and asked for a job. He said, "You're kind of puny to do a man's work." I responded, "If you give me a job and I can't do a miner's work, then tell me and I'll leave."

So he give me a job and I went to work in the mines with my granddad. The third day I heard the foreman severely criticize an old feller that by any standards today would not be able to work. I took issue with the foreman, and he promptly notified me that I could be fired for insubordination. Later my granddad said to me, "Young man, you're gonna have to curb that temper. You'll probably get fired for your action today." And I said, "Well, Granddad, I used my best judgment in trying to halt that act of disgrace to that old man. If he had jumped on you like that, I'd have probably killed him! Or at least I'd have tried it." Nothing came of it. I worked for that same foreman 15 years later in a mechanized mine and he still remembered that.

MK Tell me how blacks fared working day to day, or were there blacks on Cabin Creek? When did they first come?

AM The black people were brought in during the labor wars primarily as strike-breakers. The operators would go down South somewhere and paint these big flowery pictures about how much money you could make in mining and what kind of housing you had, which appealed to those who had primarily just come off the slave days. They would load the black people up in boxcars with food and water. And put a lock on the boxcar. They couldn't get out. They'd ride all the way to the coal camp, then they were turned loose and put to work in the mines.

It didn't take them very long to realize that these rosy pictures that was painted to them were falsehoods. They were browbeaten and treated like slaves. In some ways they were worse off than slaves, because slaves in the South, as the story's been related to me, they always managed to feed them. The blacks that come into the mining camps in the early days could scarcely make enough to feed their families. The companies assumed no responsibility for seeing that they were taken care of. And quite a lot of them, I believe, would have gone back to where they come from if they had known how to get back.

The black miner came here, not by choice. He worked in the mines. He raised a family and educated them so they would not have to work in the mines because of the way they were treated in the mines. The Mine Workers constitution has always said, "There shall be no discrimination because of race, color, or creed." But it wasn't practiced. In my early days in the mines the black miner was treated like in the South. They could have jobs hand-loading in the mines, but when automation came in, no jobs running equipment, none of the better jobs. They were discriminated against in spite of the Mine Workers constitution. They raised their children and educated them so they could find work other than the mines.

Another classic example [of people lured to the coalfields with false promises]: My great grandmother married a fellow named Jim Sullivan, an old Virginian, come out of the Blue Ridge Mountains. He came here because of all the stories he'd heard about big wages in the mines. He was a big man physically and made a very able coal miner. When I used to visit him on weekends he would set on the porch and play his fiddle and banjo and sing the old hill folk songs. One in particular was this "Blue Ridge Mountain Home." I finally listened to the words and began to understand that he would have gone back to the Blue Ridge Mountains in a minute, back to farming, if he'd a-knew how to get there, could have figured a way to get back. He didn't like it here, he didn't want to be a miner, was what he was saying in his song.

MK You said you started working in the

hand-loading days?

AM Yes. I worked for my granddad. I later worked for my brother and then my uncle in the same mine. Hand-loading. In those days, if you could get a job, you had to have somebody take you in, generally some member of the family. You worked double, two men working in the same place. It was a little harder to make extra money that way. You got paid 77 and 2/10ths cents a ton hand-loading coal when I went to work in the mines. You bought your own tools, your own powder. There was no portal-to-portal, no vacation, and no lunch period. You ate lunch when you got a chance, but you wasn't paid for it.

MK How did they measure the tons that you loaded?

AM Well, they'd run across scales and the weigh boss weighed the coal and the checkweighman checked to make sure you was given the proper weight. But it was difficult to police that operation. Sometimes they'd rig the scales, or dock you for no reason at all. They had tare boards—those are boards across the drift mouth, and if the coal on top of the car didn't touch that tare board you didn't get paid for that car of coal. That car was docked. Or if they found slate in your car they'd set it off and severely criticize you, and they wouldn't pay you for it.

MK So you were really between a rock and a hard place most of the time, no matter what you did?

AM Yeah, they had a scrip system which you were allowed to use at the company store, which you could not spend anywhere else. The company tried to get the miner in debt so he would not be able to go anywhere else. There were a few independent merchants on Cabin Creek at that time, and they always tried to harass those people, too, to keep the miner from dealing with them, because they offered better prices.

If you didn't spend your money at the company store then they would move you to rock piles or water holes, or places where you couldn't load very much coal. I experienced that myself when I first went to work. I bought a Winchester pump gun in the company store, and I agreed to pay $5.00 a payday for that gun. The first payday that I drawed after I bought the shotgun, the store manager took $10.00 out. So I went and told the store manager, "From this day forward no more scrip is to be issued on my account." That was on Friday. Monday morning when I went to work the foreman came around and said, "I'm gonna have to move you to another place." I said, "What for?" He said, "I'm the boss. And I will move you wherever I want to." The place he moved me to had 14 inches of bottom rock in the coal. You'd shoot your coal down, load it off the top, then you spent about a day cleaning up that rock, which reduced your income by quite a bit. I loaded the dust out of the place and dug out enough coal to finish loading one car. I put my tools on top and went out. That foreman came out and said, "What are you doing out here?" I said, "I just quit. I'm not gonna work for you no more."

Outside the mine superintendent said, "You're a good coal loader and a hard worker. How would you like to go up on another section and work for Johnny Bull Thompson? You'll be able to load all the coal you want to up there." I went up on that section and was given three places of seven-foot coal, no rock in it. That's the best fellow I ever worked for in the mines. And later, because he was good to his men he was fired also. Then I was back with another boss who was the same way about dealing with the company store. And they give me a water hole. I give it back to them and went to work at another mine.

I went into the service when I was 19 years old. I suffered an injury in World War II, and afterwards I tried to go back in the mines. But they still had this old graveyard principle. I went back to the superintendent of the mine where I was working before the war, and he said, "I don't have to give you a job—but I'll see if I can find you something." I went back the next evening and he said he would give me a job running duckbill* on the third [graveyard] shift.

Nobody wanted to work the third shift and he was there to make sure I got on the right mantrip. I went down in this place. It was 30 inches of coal and 10 inches of water. I sloshed around in there the one night and got that shift in. Then I told the

*The "duckbill" was an early mechanical loader.

section foreman, I said, "I want you to tell that big-nosed superintendent I'm as good a man as he is. He give me this damned job and I'm giving it back to him." I come out of the mines that night.

My brother had come up to get me and he laughed when I got into the car. I was still disgruntled about working in that water all night and I barked at him, said, "What the hell is so funny?" He said, "You know what you look like? You look like an old gob rat that somebody been trying to drown all night." I laughed, too. I said, "That's what I feel like. They been trying to drown me all night." I said, "I quit!"

Then I went to work at an automobile garage, serving out a three-year apprenticeship as auto mechanic, which prepared me to go back to the mine just when automation came in, when I worked as a repairman from then until I left the mines.

MK What was going on in your life through the late '50's?

AM Well, mining kind of fluctuated. We had problems during wartime, and after the war was over we had a very serious strike. This was just prior to Lewis allowing the industry to automate. I think the strike—this was '49 to '50—was damaging to the Mine Workers itself because it allowed the industry to automate. The membership was reduced from 600,000 to 90,000 almost overnight. There was no

provision made to compensate those who were pushed out, and I had many friends among them. They were shoved out of the mines, the only job they had. They were too old to retrain. They had to go out and migrate all over the country and accept menial tasks, cutting grass or whatever they could find. I had an uncle who went to Florida during this time and take a job as a caretaker. It was degrading for him to have to do that, to move out of his native state.

I was about to go to Florida myself, but I'd have missed these old mountains. I came to think then that it was a coward's way out for me to accept employment somewhere else. I couldn't run off and leave my friends here. I had begun then to be concerned with their plight. And I was convinced that the union had become dilatory, had no concern for its membership. At that time I was president of my local and I said to the recording secretary of the local that the Mine Workers needed leadership at the district and national levels. My friend, who later became secretary-treasurer of District 17, said, "Who's gonna clean the union up, you?" And I said, "I don't know enough about what's going on. What about yourself?" He said, "Hell, I know less about it than you do."

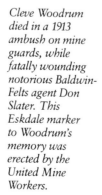

Cleve Woodrum died in a 1913 ambush on mine guards, while fatally wounding notorious Baldwin-Felts agent Don Slater. This Eskdale marker to Woodrum's memory was erected by the United Mine Workers.

For those who haven't read Denise Giardina's previous coal country novel, her new book will still offer a rich, absorbing read. But returning readers will have the added satisfaction of deepening their relationships with several families, as well as the pleasure of watching a talented writer claim a more mature and powerful voice.

The Unquiet Earth, published in May by W. W. Norton and Company, continues the story of intertwined lives in the fictional coal mining counties of Justice and Paine, on the West Virginia-Kentucky border. The novel, spanning the period from 1930 to 1990, takes up where Giardina's last book, *Storming Heaven,* ended. It is told in the voice of several narrators, some of whom are the children of characters in the earlier book.

A West Virginian raised in the coalfields, Giardina has lost none of her anger over the exploitation of her homeplace. And her book leaves no doubt about why the earth is unquiet; it has been riddled and robbed, then stripped and scarred by the greed of outsiders. Concluding as it does in contemporary times, *The Unquiet Earth* is perhaps an even stronger indictment of corporate greed and government neglect than was *Storming Heaven,* a story of the West Virginia Mine Wars.

The novelist has sharpened her powers both as a storyteller and an observer of humanity. Her characters are (and sometimes simultaneously) wise, funny, damaged, petty, stubborn, generous, real people.

The *Unquiet Earth* does not have a hero; there is no character whose virtues place him or her above all the others, no impossibly good human being. Dillon Freeman, Rachel Honaker, Rachel's daughter Jackie, Hassel Day, Tom Kolwiecki, Arthur Lee Sizemore, and their neighbors are sometimes blinded by their own frailties. They can and do make tragic mistakes, hurt one another, get on each other's nerves, get drunk, go crazy, go to jail. Like real people, they also save each other's lives, share grief and love,

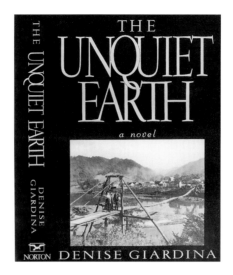

BOOK REVIEW

seek the spiritual, forgive the fallen, endure the insurmountable.

The book is divided into four sections and unfolds a saga of two generations. Much of "Book One," the first section covering more than 30 years, is narrated by Rachel Honaker and Dillon Freeman, first cousins whose illicit but undeniable love for one another weaves their two lives into a knotted tapestry. At the end of this section the reader is introduced to young Jackie, who will figure in the other compelling love story of the novel, and whose passion will echo and enlarge the stories of both Dillon and Rachel.

The pace of history slows and the story settles into its full richness in the following three sections of the novel. Book Two introduces a fourth narrator. In Hassel Day, the unofficial mayor of a coal company town called Number Thirteen, Giardina has fashioned a character who brings to mind the best creations of novelist Eudora Welty. Combining wry comedy with compassion of epic proportions, Hassel nurtures and worries over his community in a simple voice that captures the spirit of the mountains.

The character of Hassel is also a counterpoint to that of Tom Kolwiecki,

who makes his first appearance in Book Three. Both are on a spiritual quest; it's just that Hassel's quest, like his mayorship, is personal and unceremonious. If he experiences an epiphany in a pilgrimage to see a pair of dressed fleas, he is still as wise a seeker as contemporary literature offers us.

In the characters of Tom Kolwiecki and Arthur Lee Sizemore, Giardina deals with outsiders of two different types, and with the issue of fear. Tom, a VISTA volunteer, is an outsider by birth; ironically, it is his Justice County neighbors who extend to him a sense of community and a love unconditional enough to conquer his fear. Arthur Lee, in an effort to escape the poverty of his youth, has separated himself from his own people by allying himself with the coal company.

The novel brims with other memorable community members, laugh-aloud stories, and heartbreaking losses. The most important character, however, is not a human, but the earth itself. Again and again, in lyrical metaphors of blood and bone, fire and flood, Giardina sounds the central theme: the earth is somehow aware, it lives and breathes, feels pain, holds memories, and avenges wrong. Its fate and that of its inhabitants, like the lives played out in Number Thirteen, are inextricably bound together.

Giardina speaks of this through the voice of narrator Dillon Freeman: ". . . they are not just piles of rock, they are ancient spirits. The old ones believed that way, my people used to say, and so do the Indians in this country. I knew it myself when I worked in the mine. I could hear the mountain above me groan and cry out, mourning its losses, screaming with pain when we cut away its bones. I knew when the roof fell and took a man it was no accident but the mountain lashing out like a wounded animal."

—Colleen Anderson

The Unquiet Earth *is available as a $5.99 paperback in bookstores, or through the order form on page 109.*

AUTHOR BIOGRAPHIES

R.B. ADAMS, now retired, worked in the engineering departments of U.S. Coal & Coke Company in Gary, West Virginia, and the Island Creek Coal Company in Holden. He was also purchasing agent at the Boone County Coal Corporation.

COLLEEN ANDERSON is a poet, writer and graphic designer. She owns Mother Wit, a Charleston design firm, and has done work for GOLDENSEAL since its inception. Originally from Michigan, she came to West Virginia in 1970 as a VISTA worker and helped organize Cabin Creek Quilts, a quilting cooperative.

HARRY M. BRAWLEY, a Charleston native, was born in 1909. He has worked for WCHS Radio in Charleston, as a teacher and principal in Kanawha County, and as a part-time professor at Morris Harvey College. He has published widely and was a member of the Charleston City Council.

BOB & CAROLE DAMRON, from Logan and Charleston respectively, wrote and produced "Brimstone and Lace," the Mother Jones play excerpted in this GOLDENSEAL book. It was presented at Charleston's Mother Jones Festival in 1980.

MICHAEL KLINE spent childhood summers in Hampshire County and later worked in various poverty programs in Kentucky and West Virginia. Kline, assistant editor of GOLDENSEAL in 1978, is now a public folklorist with the Pioneer Valley Folklore Society in Greenfield, Massachusetts.

BIRDIE BLEDSOE KYLE grew up in Fayette County and on Cabin Creek in Kanawha County. She now works for Congressman Nick Rahall in Washington and says West Virginia is never far from her thoughts.

LOIS C. MCLEAN, a long-time student of West Virginia labor history, is an acknowledged authority on the life of Mother Jones. She serves as president of the Raleigh County Historic Landmark Commission.

MICHAEL M. MEADOR, born in Hinton and raised in Princeton, recently graduated from the West Virginia School of Osteopathic Medicine. He has a long-standing interest in the history of southern West Virginia.

J. RODERICK MOORE, a native of Fincastle, Virginia, was raised in Welch. He is now director of the Blue Ridge Institute at Ferrum College in Virginia.

JOSEPH PLANTANIA is a Huntington native and freelance writer. He has written widely on the history of southern West Virginia and the Ohio Valley.

JOE W. SAVAGE, born in Charleston in 1897, worked as a reporter for the *Charleston Gazette* in the 1920's. Mr. Savage, a freelance writer, died in 1974.

LON SAVAGE is the author of the popular Mine Wars book, *Thunder in the Mountains*, and the son of Joe Savage. He worked ten years as a newspaperman for the *Richmond Times-Dispatch* and as a bureau chief for United Press International. Lon Savage was a tank commander in Europe in the early 1950's.

TOPPER SHERWOOD, a Charleston freelance writer, came to West Virginia when less than a year old. He has worked at the *Charleston Gazette*, the *Charleston Daily Mail* and the Associated Press, and has had articles published in *Time* and the *Boston Globe*.

GORDON LLOYD SWARTZ III, a native West Virginian, has been a coal miner at Consolidation Coal's Shoemaker Mine in Marshall County for 17 years. He is the father of five children, including the largest set of twins ever born in West Virginia.

RICK WILSON grew up in Milton. He is a freelance writer and co-author of the book, *Blenko Glass 1930–1950*. He was assistant director of the Putnam County Library, and now serves as project director of the American Friends Service Committee's Economic Justice Project in Charleston.

Biographical information current as of September 1991.

BIBLIOGRAPHY

Corbin, David Alan. *Life, Work, and Rebellion in the Coal Fields: The Southern West Virginia Miners*, 1880–1922. Chicago: University of Illinois Press, 1981.

_____, editor. *The West Virginia Mine Wars: An Anthology*. Charleston: Appalachian Editions, 1991.

Fetherling, Dale. *Mother Jones, the Miners' Angel: A Portrait*. Carbondale: Southern Illinois University Press, 1974.

Giardina, Denise. *Storming Heaven*. New York: W. W. Norton & Company, 1987.

Jones, Mary Harris. *The Autobiography of Mother Jones*. Edited by Mary Field Parton. Chicago: Charles H. Kerr Publishing Company, 1976.

Lee, Howard B. *Bloodletting in Appalachia*. Parsons, West Virginia: McClain Printing Company, 1969.

Lunt, Richard D. *Law and Order vs. The Miners: West Virginia, 1907–1933*. Hamden, Connecticut: Archon Books, 1979.

Mooney, Fred. *Struggle in the Coal Fields: The Autobiography of Fred Mooney*. Edited by J. W. Hess. Morgantown: West Virginia University Library, 1967.

Savage, Lon. *Thunder in the Mountains: The West Virginia Mine War 1920–21*. Pittsburgh: University of Pittsburgh Press, 1990.

Sayles, John. *Thinking in Pictures: The Making of the Movie Matewan*. Boston: Houghton Mifflin Company, 1987.

Settle, Mary Lee. *Scapegoat*. New York: Charles Scribner's Sons, 1988.

Steel, Edward M. *The Correspondence of Mother Jones*. Pittsburgh: University of Pittsburgh Press, 1985.

_____. *The Speeches and Writings of Mother Jones*. Pittsburgh: University of Pittsburgh Press, 1988.

Vol. 22, No. 2 • WEST VIRGINIA TRADITIONAL LIFE • Summer 1996 • $3.95

Goldenseal

Bringing the
Steel Driver
Home

Family Fun in
Preston County

Cool by the Pool

Summer Camp

And More!

JOHN HENRY

1996

ABOUT **Goldenseal** . . .

GOLDENSEAL magazine celebrates West Virginia's industrial heritage, folklife, and recent history four times a year. Featuring articles from across the state, GOLDENSEAL is based on the recollections of living West Virginians, beautifully illustrated with archival and recent photography.

This attractive, 72-page quarterly is published by the State of West Virginia. Since 1975, GOLDENSEAL has brought true-life stories of West Virginia to print like no other publication. In addition to the fascinating collection of mine wars stories reprinted here, GOLDENSEAL has published hundreds of unique articles over the years. Topics include traditional music, farming practices, religion, family histories, crafts, ethnic communities, logging, architecture, herbs, sports, politics, and dozens of other subjects.

In addition, GOLDENSEAL gives up-to-date information on folklife activities around the state; notices of recently released books, recordings, films, and videos about West Virginia; and a comprehensive listing of upcoming fairs and festivals.

It's easy to keep up with all of this, simply by becoming a GOLDENSEAL subscriber. For $16 a year, you can have GOLDENSEAL mailed directly to your home or office. Or give GOLDENSEAL as a gift to someone else who loves West Virginia as much as you do!

As a SPECIAL OFFER, if you subscribe to GOLDENSEAL through this edition of *The GOLDENSEAL Book of the West Virginia Mine Wars*, you will receive a FREE copy of the commemorative Mother Jones issue of the magazine (October–December 1980) with your paid subscription. Simply clip or photocopy the form below, check the appropriate box, and send it in with your $16 check, and we will send your FREE magazine. (Hurry! Offer good while supplies last.) Your subscription will start with the next issue.

You may also write to us at The Cultural Center, 1900 Kanawha Blvd. East, Charleston, WV 25305-0300; or phone us at (304) 558-0220 and request this SPECIAL OFFER.

Date _____

Yes! I want to receive the best of West Virginia traditional culture in each issue of GOLDENSEAL.

☐ I am enclosing $16.   ☐ Please send my FREE Mother Jones issue.

PLEASE SEND MAGAZINES TO:

Name _____

Address _____

City, State, ZIP_____

MAKE CHECKS PAYABLE TO GOLDENSEAL.

MAIL TO GOLDENSEAL, The Cultural Center
1900 Kanawha Blvd., East, Charleston, WV 25305-0300

Mary Harris "Mother" Jones is a legend in the history of organized labor, and is especially remembered for her work in West Virginia. An ardent advocate for the rights of working people, Mother Jones was tireless in her efforts to organize unions across the country. She was also a feisty and colorful individual. Over the years, Mother Jones has made many appearances in the pages of GOLDENSEAL and much of that material is reprinted in our *Mine Wars* book.

In addition, GOLDENSEAL devoted its October–December 1980 issue (Volume 6, Number 4) to Mother Jones to commemorate the 50th anniversary of her death in 1930 when, by her own count, she had reached 100 years of age.

The 1980 special issue of GOLDENSEAL features a Mother Jones portrait on the cover and a Mother Jones theme, with stories pertaining to this famous agitator and West Virginia's labor and industrial history.

Other articles include *Florien Vaughn, M.D., Mystery Doctor of the Coalfields* by Lawton W. Posey with Bryson R. Posey; *The Monongah Miners' Band* by Lois C. McLean, *Coal Town Baseball* by Paul J. Nyden, and a photo essay on McDowell County by Doug Yarrow. With other GOLDENSEAL stories and features from around the state, this magazine is a well-rounded, collectable edition.

GOLDENSEAL still has a limited number of these special Mother Jones issues available, while supplies last. As a SPECIAL OFFER, the Mother Jones issue is free to new GOLDENSEAL subscribers using the form on page 107. Subscriptions are $16 a year.

The issue is also available from the GOLDENSEAL office for $3.95 a copy plus $1 shipping.

To order, make checks payable to GOLDENSEAL. Mail to GOLDENSEAL, The Cultural Center, 1900 Kanawha Blvd., East, Charleston, WV 25305-0300; or phone (304)558-0220.

PICTORIAL HISTORIES DISTRIBUTION
specializing in West Virginia books

If you enjoyed *The Goldenseal Book of the West Virginia Mine Wars,* you may be interested in other books about the mine wars and coal mining in West Virginia. Pictorial Histories Distribution specializes in books about West Virginia, carrying over 250 different titles. Listed below are the titles we carry which tell the tale of the West Virginia Mine Wars.

Storming Heaven by Denise Giardinia
(paperback) $5.99

Unquiet Earth by Denise Giardinia
(paperback) $5.99

Thunder In The Mountains by Lon Savage
(trade paperback) $14.95

Matewan by John Sayles
(video) $19.95

Bloodletting In Appalachia by Howard B. Lee
(trade paperback) $9.95

Law and Order vs. The Miners: West Virginia 1906–1933 by Richard Lunt
(trade paperback) $12.95

Life, Work, and Rebellion in the Coal Fields:
The Southern West Virginia Miners, 1880–1922 by David Alan Corbin
(trade paperback) $14.95

The West Virginia Mine Wars: An Anthology by David Alan Corbin
(trade paperback) $9.95

John L. Lewis: A Biography by Melvyn Dubofsky and Warren Van Tine
(trade paperback) $16.95

If you are interested in ordering any of the above titles, contact us at:
PICTORIAL HISTORIES DISTRIBUTION
1416 Quarrier Street, Charleston, WV 25301
tel 304-342-1848   fax 304-343-0594

Please include $3.50 shipping for the first item, and .50 for each additional item. West Virginia residents must add 6 % sales tax. We accept Visa and Mastercard, and ship within 48 hours. Ask for a complete list of our titles, if interested.